My Dearest Darling

My Dearest Darling

Letters of Love in Wartime

Edited and Annotated by

Lisa Franco

July 7, 2018
Margery Storey's Committal Service

Down a grassy path, under an arbor, and into a shady secret garden at St. Mary's Church in Barnstable, Massachusetts, a single ray of sunlight shines directly into a perfectly square hollow in the ground. Quietly and reverently, family members gather as a tow-headed toddler clutching a daisy curiously peers into the final resting place of Margery Eleanor Stickles Storey. A nearby sign lists the other souls buried here. Among them is Margery's husband, Donald Edgar Storey.

The scene described above could have marked the end of a love story.
Instead, this book is its resurrection.

Table of Contents

Preface

—— ❧ ——

Something drew me to the laundry basket in the musty basement of the Cape Cod antique shop in the spring of 2011. As I approached, I noticed a simple handwritten sign: World War II Ephemera. I knelt down and found several letters in airmail envelopes. I reached in, picked one up, read it, and began to weep.

I'd discovered a treasure trove of love letters, more than 150, written during World War II by a young sailor, Donald Edgar Storey, and his sweetheart, Margery Eleanor Stickles, who later became his wife. They began many of their messages to each other with the sweetest salutation: "My Dearest Darling." Mixed in with the letters were photos of Donald in his U.S. Navy uniform, deployment papers, wartime food ration stamps, dance cards, and other relics.

I left the shop without buying the contents of the basket, but could not get them out of my mind that night. I returned the next day, made an offer, and took them home, vowing to preserve and protect them. A nearly perfect window into history, the letters were full of passion, hope, and longing. I knew almost immediately I wanted to share them publicly—partly because of my journalism background, and partly because they touched me so deeply. But first I had to find the family, earn their trust, and get their permission to compile and publish this book.

The process took more than a decade. Along the way, I learned that Donald had died four years before I found the letters. Margery was still alive, but she had moved away from Cape Cod.

With the help of an amateur sleuth who had a flair for Census documents, I tracked Margery down in 2014. She was 91 and living in upstate New York with one of her three children, Don Jr., and his wife Vicky. At their invitation, I traveled to meet them that October. Margery seemed happy and content at her son's house, though her memory was fading. But she still had some connections to her past: When the Army vs. Navy football game came on television, she knew which team to root for.

The family told me they held an estate sale after Donald's death, but never meant to sell the letters. Someone must have inadvertently put them in with the sale items. While they were surprised to learn I had them, they gave their blessing for me to pursue this project.

A few years after I met her, Margery passed away. She died not knowing of my intentions, in accordance with her family's wishes. I attended her internment ceremony the following summer and read one of her letters during the service. As I voiced Margery's words to her family, I was overcome with emotion. The connection I felt to this couple was strong, though I'd only gotten to know them through their letters.

Determined to preserve the legacy of Donald and Margery's love, I continued working on the book after Margery's death. The final product details how World War II, and the circumstances surrounding it, shaped the lives of two young people who were mad about each other. Theirs is the story of a tumultuous, yet simpler time in America. Were it not for a little bit of luck, it might have been lost forever.

Introduction

During the Second World War (1939–1945), letters were the primary means of communication between those who served overseas and their loved ones on the home front. They lifted morale, and helped them feel more connected to home. They were filled not only with day-to-day news, but often contained deeply personal messages mingled with longing for a brighter future.[1] Today, this carefully penned correspondence is not only historic, but priceless, as letter writing seems to be a lost art.

The letters in this book were written and mailed between 1941 and 1947. They chronicle the budding romance and the first four years of marriage of naval officer Donald Storey and his sweetheart Margery. The couple spent most of this time apart due to Donald's involvement in the Pacific Ocean theater of the war. Even in peacetime, his naval service kept them from each other for another two years. Throughout that time, he wrote to Margery almost every day, and she likely wrote back just as frequently, though only eight of her letters survived. Consequently, nearly all of the messages published in this book are from Donald. They exist today because Margery kept them safe after opening them. Though her voice appears far less in these pages, it is because of her devotion to Donald that we have such a robust record of their correspondence.

Donald, also known as Don, was born in Mt. Vernon, New York, on March 15, 1922. Margery, who went by Mardy, was born the following year on February 4. They grew up in the same neighborhood, but the pair didn't start courting until 1941, the year Donald enrolled at the United States Naval Academy in Annapolis, Maryland. At the time, Mardy was attending Mary Washington College in Fredericksburg, Virginia. According to their family, Donald needed a date for a dance one night, and because he knew Mardy from home, he asked her to go with him. They began exchanging letters around this time.

It was not uncommon for letters to be lost or delayed in transit. It could be months before they arrived at their destination, often in large bundles. As a result, there were sometimes long gaps in time when Donald and Mardy did not hear from each other, making each letter even more precious.

Donald moved around a lot during his years in the service. After graduating from the academy in June 1943, he first served on a destroyer, the USS *Gatling*, and then on a submarine, the USS *Carbonero*. In his final assignment, he served as commanding officer of the *LST-642*, a tank landing ship. Mardy, meanwhile, mostly stayed with her family, finding work as a secretary after leaving college early. She would have no knowledge of Donald's whereabouts or safety until a parcel of his messages arrived on her doorstep—but even then, she was not privy to certain particulars.

The government censored these letters to protect classified information, anything that could give away a location or battle plans. For this reason, Donald omitted many details about his deployments in his letters from the Pacific. While his messages didn't contain any government redactions, it was tough to figure out where he was writing from. To approximate his locations, I used internet sources that document the historical itinerary for each of his vessels and cross-referenced those with the dates he printed at the top of his letters. However, he didn't always include a date in his earliest letters, so whenever possible I used the postmarks found on the airmail envelopes accompanying most of those. In a few cases, the postmarks were badly smudged or faded, making it difficult to date the letters with precision.

The 135 letters I have included here have been lightly edited for content and clarity, but I've left many of the couple's typos and inconsistencies to preserve the spontaneous character of their writing. I have also included notes explaining military terms, pop culture references, and historical events that modern readers might not recognize. For privacy purposes, I have not used the full surnames of most friends and acquaintances mentioned in the letters. Additionally, in most cases I have not included full addresses.

With the help of Donald and Mardy's children—Marcy, who was born during the war and is referenced in many of the letters as "T'Nook," and Don Jr. and Christopher, who were born in peacetime—I have stitched together details from the young couple's lives that their letters do not mention. Most letters include a brief introduction with some background about what was going on in their world at the time of writing. Notes are sometimes included when additional details are needed to understand events described in the letters, though many times a lack of surviving information makes further explanation impossible. Some information has simply been lost in time.

PART ONE

CHAPTER ONE

Courtship and Engagement

The following is the earliest surviving letter between the couple. Donald composed it when he was a Naval Academy student and Mardy was at college in nearby Virginia. He sent it less than two months before Japan's attack on Pearl Harbor, on December 7, 1941, after which the United States officially entered the war. You can feel his growing love for her at this early stage in their relationship, despite his formal writing.

DE Storey
4459 Bancroft Hall*
U.S.N.A., Annapolis, Md.

Miss Mardy Stickles
Mary Washington College
Fredericksburg
Va.

[Postmarked October 27, 1941]
Sunday
[Letter not dated]

Darling –
I hope that by this time you have received my letters. If not, there is

something radically wrong with the postal system. We seem to have quite some trouble with our letters.

Darling, I certainly missed you this weekend. I really was a sad apple at the hop** last night, and it is the last time I'll ever stag it. I saw two good shows over the weekend – "Honky Tonk" and "A Yank in the R.A.F."*** Those and the hop complete the list of my activities. I saw Alice at the dance last night and she asked to be remembered to you. Did you have a good weekend?

Next weekend we go to Philadelphia for the Penn game. After what Navy did yesterday I'm afraid we may get beaten. We are getting 7 o'clock liberty after the game. That won't be much time, but it's better than nothing. I have to go chow now, and will continue after.

Angel, I just tried to reach you on the phone. The number was busy, so I'll try again around ten. I'm all settled down at my desk ready to begin work for another week. What a life!

Darling, I hope you'll write a bit oftener. There seems to be a long interval between letters. I miss you like the devil.

All my love,

Don

P.S. Love you just a little bit

Darling – Here's a good target for darts. I hope you never want to throw darts at it.****

---

*Bancroft Hall is a massive dormitory complex at Annapolis that houses all the school's students, who are called midshipmen.[1]

**A hop or sock hop was a dance party for young people, where many of the dancers went shoeless.[2]

****Honky Tonk* is a 1941 romance movie starring Clark Gable and Lana Turner, who were huge screen stars of the time. [3] *A Yank in the R.A.F.* is a1941 film starring Tyrone Power and Betty Grable,[4] whose iconic 1943 pinup pose adorned soldiers' barracks worldwide during World War II. [5]

****Donald sometimes included photos of himself with his letters, and he could be referring to one here. But there was no picture in the envelope found with this letter.

No letters survived from the rest of 1941 or 1942. The next letter from Donald to Mardy is from January 1943, shortly after she paid him a visit at Annapolis. By this time, the couple had become engaged to be married after Donald's proposal a week earlier on Christmas Day. Mardy was back home in Mt. Vernon, having left school before graduating so her sister could attend college. This decision was most likely due to family finances.

Donald's writing had become more casual, though he felt self-conscious about putting into words how he felt about his new fiancé. He figured it out by the end of his letter, even closing with a pet name for her.

Midn.* DE Storey, U.S.N.
4301 Bancroft Hall
Annapolis, Maryland

Miss Mardy Stickles
Mount Vernon
New York

[Postmarked January 3, 1943]
Sunday
[Letter not dated]

Darling –

One more perfect weekend gone. We have had quite a number of them in the last two years, but everyone seems to have a little something added that its predecessor lacked.

As usual, I despised saying goodbye and as soon as you left I rushed over and bought a great big Coke in which I drowned my sorrows. Pink lips and all! Since then I have been sitting here and daydreaming of you and just thinking about all the little things – like the way you smile all over – which make me love you so deeply.

Sometimes I feel like an awful stoop. Do I say much that seems funny and out of place? I always want so much to tell you how I feel about you, and then when I begin I seem to get tongue tied. I think that I will practice nightly on your picture.

You looked so sweet in your blue dress this afternoon that I could have hugged you for hours and hours, but the galloping goose** had to claim you at 5:15. Aren't you glad you didn't take that 1:15 train? Be honest now!

Hope you had a decent trip back and that you didn't have any ill effects from going breakfastless. You really do need someone to look after you, darling, and I am and will always be making a strong bid for that job.

At present, I am planning on the first weekend in February and if nothing goes astray, I will meet you in Penn station. I can stay with my aunt, so don't go to any trouble on that score. Anyhow that is three weeks off so perhaps we shouldn't count our chickens before they hatch.

I am not looking forward to tomorrow with a great deal of zest, but I've done it many times before so I guess this Monday will not do me in either.

It is bed time angel, and though for some strange reason I am not the least bit tired tonight, there appears to be nothing I can do but hit the hay.

Give my love to your folks, but keep loads for yourself. I miss you terribly and love you so much that every sound I hear seems to whisper: Mardy, Mardy, Mardy.

Until tomorrow - I'll go on loving "Snookie Puddin"

Don

XXXXX

---

*Midshipman

**A tongue-in-cheek name for a train. The Galloping Geese were a series of unique railcars that operated in Colorado during this time.[6]

Sunday –

Darling –

One more perfect weekend gone. We have had quite a number of them in the last two years, but every one seems to have a little something added that its predecessor lacked.

As usual, I despised saying goodbye and as soon as you left I rushed over and bought a great big coke in which I drowned my sorrows. Pink lips and all! Had a lecture by a lad out of '42 after chow tonight. Since then I have been sitting here and day dreaming of you and just thinking about all the little things – like the way you smile all over – which make me love you so deeply.

The couple's rendezvous were rare, and phone calls were sporadic. Donald often pined for Mardy in his letters, as he did in the following message. By this point, they had realized letters could arrive out of sequence, and Donald would sometimes number his messages so Mardy could eventually read groups of them in the order in which they were written.

[No address information available]

Jan. 4, 1943

15

My Dearest Darling –

Perhaps this may not get mailed for ten days or so, but I'm going to pile the letters up so that when they do get mailed there will be a goodly pack. I'm on the beach at present – at school! I imagine I'll be here for 10 days, and I'm not complaining! 'Tis a very desolate spot but the sleep is good and there is an ice box stocked with beer. Too bad I couldn't have gotten some of this beach duty about a month or so ago!

Angel, I dream and plan every day of that wonderful day when we can "set up housekeeping". Hope I'll be able to wear nice Harris tweeds at that time also. Darling, do you realize that since you and I became "one" we've only been together for three days. The nights were far more numerous for which I am duly thankful, but the days were far too few.

Heard our song tonight on the Bing Crosby program* and I held a one man séance in which I thought very hard and put myself by your side – very, very close by your side! There is no place on earth I would rather be than with you. This world is a big and a beautiful place but it's just no go when you are not with me. Thank goodness I've lived a true bachelor's life for a few years with few and rare diversions. If I hadn't I think I would go stark raving mad now that I've had a taste – small but sweet – of what a wonderful proposition loving you is.

I guess this is all for tonight. My love to your folks. I love you so very much and guess you know by now how much I want to be with you forever.

Forever yours,

Don

---

*Donald and Mardy's song was "As Time Goes By," which became famous for its use in the 1942 movie *Casablanca*.[7] Bing Crosby was an American star of epic proportion, with combined talents including singing and acting. When the U.S. War Department established the Armed Forces Radio Service in 1942, Bing was a regular performer on the network's programs. [8]

In this letter, Donald longed for his sweetheart in the wake of one of their visits. He also expressed concern for her father's health, a gesture that indicates how important her family had become to him.

Midn. DE Storey, U.S.N.
4301 Bancroft Hall
Annapolis, Maryland

Miss Mardy Stickles
Mount Vernon
New York

[Postmarked January 15, 1943]
Thursday
[Letter not dated]

Darling –

When you get this it will be after we have said another goodbye. Hope you had a good trip back!

Right now I'm sitting here listening to Gene Krupa* and thinking of one person. Gosh but I'll be glad to see you darling. At present, I'm contemplating on how I can persuade you to just stay down here. Those trips are long and hard.

Sorry to hear about your dad, and I hope he'll be up and mixing when you open this. That bronchitis stuff isn't any fun. It can certainly make you feel mighty low.

Did I say that time makes everything easier – well right now I find no solace in that little bit of philosophy. This has been just about the slowest week I can ever remember. Even the seconds drag by!

Angel, this is one sailor who only has one port and one girl in it. There is one and only one girl in the world for me and I'll give you three guesses as to who it can be.

Darling, I hope that when you open this it will be after a good weekend. Miss you more and more all the time and love you something terrific.

Forever yours,

Don

---

*Gene Krupa was a superstar American jazz drummer and band leader. [9]

With the promise of another meeting on the horizon, Donald was very excited and seemed to enjoy planning an itinerary. As an endearing sign of his affection, he crafted this letter, knowing Mardy wouldn't receive it until after their visit.

According to this letter, it looks as if Mardy had taken a job as a secretary at this point.

Midn. DE Storey, U.S.N.
4301 Bancroft Hall
Annapolis, Maryland

Miss Mardy Stickles
Mount Vernon
New York

[Postmarked January 16, 1943]
Friday
[Letter not dated]

Darling –

Yippie, at this time tomorrow night I will be with you. We are even going to try and get something to eat at Carvel Hall* tomorrow night. Hope it works out better than last time.

Sorry to hear that you weren't feeling up to par. Guess that is a delayed reaction from the hectic Christmas Day. However, I'll see you tomorrow and will get the whole story.

I feel so good tonight just knowing that tomorrow afternoon I'll be able to look at, talk with, and walk with my "snuggly wuggly". Gosh but this has been a long week. Seems to me that I have said that quite a few times before.

Have lots to tell you tomorrow so I'll save it 'til then. Just wanted you to have a letter when you got home from the office Monday night.

Love you very much and miss you more than anything.

Forever Yours,

Don

---

*Carvel Hall was Annapolis' grandest hotel, where Naval Academy cadets often socialized. [10]

Based on the following correspondence, mailed only three days later, it seems as if the couple's rendezvous may have not taken place. As Donald mentioned in his previous letter, Mardy hadn't been feeling well. Could it be she was still ill?

Midn. DE Storey, U.S.N.
4301 Bancroft Hall
Annapolis, Md.

Miss Mardy Stickles
Mount Vernon
N.Y.

[Postmarked January 19, 1943]
Monday
[Letter not dated]

Darling –

Woke up this morning to the tune of that belated rain. Glad it didn't come over the weekend. I don't care what kind of weather we have during the week. Spent a very long day in classes and grabbed an hour's sleep this afternoon.

Right now I'm listening to the Coca Cola program. It is coming from Camp Sampson, that navy training station your father was telling us about in upper New York State. Sounds as if they have quite a large group of men up there.

For some strange reason, I have been wishing all night that I were sitting in front of a warm fire light with you.

I will be much happier when I once again can look forward to a letter in the mornings. I noticed its absence very much this morning.

Well, angel, the sands of time are once again running out. I miss you more than ever and love you twice as much as I miss you.

Forever yours,

Don

Before writing this next message, Donald received a letter from Mardy's mother containing further news about her illness. Mardy was suffering from appendicitis! Donald was vexed that he couldn't tend to her himself and felt restless with worry over her condition. Though Mardy would make a full recovery, the situation foreshadowed the constant worry and doubt the couple would face once Donald graduated and went off to war.

Midn. DE Storey, USN
4301 Bancroft Hall
Annapolis, Maryland

Miss Mardy Stickles
Mount Vernon
New York

[Postmarked January 30, 1943]
Saturday
[Letter not dated]

Darling –

I'm hoping for all I'm worth that by the time you receive this that the appendicitis attack will be a dim memory. I certainly am sorry, and I would have given anything to have been able to run over and see you today instead of having to telephone. I am the world's worst on a phone to boot.

Darling, you hurry up and get well before next Saturday! I am counting on next weekend so much. If, perchance, you have had it yanked when this reaches you – so much the better (in a way), at least you won't ever have to give the darn thing another thought. Also, if next weekend is spoiled, remember that there are plenty more – 52 in a year!

I hope I didn't wake anyone when I called this morning. I had been up for hours, so I didn't stop to realize that it was a fairly early hour for civilized folk – especially on a "no work" Saturday. As soon as I opened your mom's grand letter, I knew that I had to call and find out how you were or I wouldn't rest easy. I'm still not resting too easy, but talking to snookie certainly made me feel loads better.

Angel, being midnight, it is way past my bedtime. I'm going to quit now, but will write a long long letter tomorrow.

I love you very much, darling and will pray extra specially tonight that next Saturday at this time you will be asleep on my shoulder as the train rolls onward to Fleetwood* (ever a local!)

Forever yours,

Don

OXXXXXXXXXXO

---

*Fleetwood train station, Mt. Vernon, New York.

In this letter, Donald shared some summer vacation plans with Mardy and hoped she could join him at a lake house where he would be staying with a group of friends and their parents.

Midn. DE Storey, U.S.N.
4301 Bancroft Hall
Annapolis, Md.

Miss Mardy Stickles
Mount Vernon
New York

[Postmarked February, 1943, day indistinguishable]
Sunday
[Letter not dated]

Darling –

Tonight is worse than London in the fall, or something. Anyhow it is so foggy that you can't see your hand before your face. Spent the usual Sunday. Spaghetti and the movies, with Ev.* Ev and I also made arrangements for June Week.**

Just came up from the phone. You don't know how happy I am to know that you are all right. Now I really cannot wait until Saturday. This week will certainly drag. However, when the end finally comes it will bring the best thing in the world with it.

I started to tell you about June Week. We have a house out on Weem's Creek. It is quite large with a nice big porch and a lawn right down to the water. It is fairly far out, so we will have some walking to do. There will be King's mother, Ev's parents, mother and dad, Connie,*** and I hope – you.

What a spooky story is on the radio right now. Don't think I will sleep too soundly tonight. Perhaps thinking of you will make me fall asleep and have beautiful dreams.

I was just told that I have the morning exercises this week. More fun, especially when one is as sleepy as I in the morning. I'll really put the boys through their paces.

Right now I'm listening to Winchell.**** He certainly doesn't pull his punches. Right now he is giving congress he – –.

Darling, I'm not feeling any too hot tonight, so if you'll please excuse me I'm going to hit the hay. Love you always.

Forever,

Don

XXXXXXXX

---

*Ev was a good friend of Donald's who appears several times throughout these letters.

**Annapolis' term for graduation week, "June Week" is also used by West Point and the U.S. Air Force Academy.[11]

***Connie was Ev's girlfriend, later his wife.

****Walter Winchell was an American gossip columnist whose syndicated newspaper columns and radio broadcasts were widely popular at this time. [12]

In two days, it would be Valentine's Day, and Donald's love letter to Mardy began with a little rhyme—a sweet intimation of how much he missed her. He also seemed disappointed he wasn't able to send her a nicer card.

Midn. DE Storey, USN
4301 Bancroft Hall
Annapolis, Md.

Miss Mardy Stickles
Mount Vernon
N.Y.

[Postmarked February 12, 1943]
Thursday
[Letter not dated]

Darling "buggy" –

For my valentine I pine – and how. How are you these days, angel mine? Miss me a little now and then? 'Twas sort of a sorry valentine I sent to my best gal, but it is the best one can do in this town of all towns.

Tomorrow night I will not be able to write as we have a combat problem over across the Severn.* Bet it will be mighty cold. I'll let you in on the confidential dope. The zero hour is 2100 and Don's platform has to capture objective no. 2. Only trouble is we're only using blanks.

I almost called you up again tonight, but discretion proved the better part of valor and I didn't do it. It was so nice talking to you last night. I figure we'll have a long talk about things and such tonight – in my dreams – so I won't lose out entirely.

Good night, love. I miss you more than ever and love you just a weeney bit more than I did last night.

Forever and ever and ever,

Donnie

XXXXXXXX

---

*The Severn River, where Donald likely took part in combat drills with the other midshipmen. The U.S. Naval Academy campus sits at the river's mouth.

No letters survived between mid-February and the beginning of June 1943. The following was written seven days before Donald's graduation. He was in the midst of celebrating; having had plenty of beer before sitting down to write, but even his high spirits couldn't mask his uncertainty about the future. He didn't know where his upcoming deployment would be, and he was concerned about how much distance it might put between them.

Midn. DE Storey, USN
4301 Bancroft Hall
Annapolis, Md.

Miss Mardy Stickles
Mount Vernon
N.Y.

[Postmarked June 2, 1943]
Tuesday
[Letter not dated]

Darling –

I hope I wasn't too bad over the phone tonight, and I also hope you can make this out. At present, I am feeling just grand. However, guess I can't take it anymore as all I've had is beer.

As I told you, I will be on a new call. I don't know what coast, but I'm hoping it will be east. I love you so much that I don't know whether I could take Pacific duty. I may be feeling mellow, but there is one thing I'm always sure of and that is my love for you.

Sorry I missed you earlier in the evening. I was a bit dubious about calling so early, but I decided to take a chance. Enjoyed talking to your mom, but as usual I was a very dull conversationalist.

Darling, I hope you won't get mad at this letter. I do love you so very much my sweet, and can't wait to be with you again.

Forever yours,

Don

XOXOXO

CHAPTER TWO

Post-Graduation

Donald got his wish—at least temporarily—to be stationed on the East Coast after graduation. The Navy awarded him the rank of ensign and assigned him to spend the next several months training at the Naval Air Station in Jacksonville, Florida, before sending him to the Pacific. Because of the war, the academy accelerated courses and graduated his class a year early, on June 9, 1943; however, in his letters, he correctly referred to himself as a member of the class of 1944.

Ensign DE Storey, USN
Sixth Company – Class 1944
NAS, Jacksonville, Fla.

Miss Mardy Stickles
Mount Vernon
New York

> [Postmarked June 30, 1943]
> Tuesday
> [Letter not dated]

Darling –
Another one of those nice warm days gone by. However, this is one easy life

and I'm not complaining at all. Just finished a swim and dinner. There is a honey of a pool here. I'm going to walk over and have a drink in a minute or so, and then I'm going to camp by the phone until I hear your voice. I have a fist full of change, and the connections had better be clear.

Pardon me for saying so, sweets, but the letter I received today was quite formal. None of that now!

Hey, snooks, whatever happened to those pictures? I have been expecting them daily, and I feel every letter to see how fat it is and always no soap. Don't forget to send them or I'll run up and scratch your chin. I'll do that anyhow if you'll let me.

This is quite some base. There are over 100,000 people on the base and just thousands of buildings and airplanes. Plenty of "fly boys" too, but they seem like a very regular bunch of fellows. Saw Dick B. for awhile this afternoon. He's second pilot of one of the PBY's* out here – mean anything to you? It didn't to me until two weeks ago. I am at least beginning to know one plane from another now, but that's about the limit of my learnin' thus far. We spent all day sitting on our sitters and hearing fellas talk about seaplane recovery, etc. This stuff is all very interesting, but doubt very much if I would care for flying as a steady diet.

I think Ev and I are going down to St. Augustine for the day next Sunday. It is one of the oldest cities in the United States, has a nice beach, and is not overcrowded with the uniforms. It's fun to go to new places, but would be so much more fun if you were with me. You and I are going to have to see a lot of this old world together. How about it?

Angel, give my best to the folks. I'm going to go have my nightly daiquiri and then tackle the telephone. Here's hoping!

Love and Kisses,

Don

P.S. In case I don't reach you on the telephone, I love you again tonight!

---

*During the war, the Navy relied heavily on the amphibious Consolidated PBY Catalina plane for long-range patrols, attacks and search-and-rescues.[1]

By August, Donald had moved to a different naval air station in Melbourne, Florida. He and Mardy were looking forward to an important vacation together. The trip, which Donald wrote about excitedly in the following letter, would kick off later in the month. But he couldn't help mentioning that his first ship deployment would begin right after. Even as the couple tried to enjoy their romance, they never escaped the reality of war.

DE Storey, Ens., USN
Sixth Co. – Class 1944
U.S. Naval Air Station
Melbourne, Florida

Miss Mardy Stickles
Mount Vernon
N.Y.

[Postmarked August 12, 1943]
Wednesday
[Letter not dated]

Darling –

It won't be long now. You'd better start believing that I'll be taking advantage of your hospitality or else you'll be in for a big surprise on August 22nd.

Looks like we're going to be busy keeping up with our social calendar, but we're going to have more than one night absolutely alone when we can do all the talking you want to.

Spent the afternoon at the beach again. It certainly is going to be hard to get down to brass tacks and do a little work, but I'll be doing it or else a month from now.

I got in a poker game last night and lost two-fifty, so guess I'll have to sit in again and see how my luck's running tonight. That old saying "unlucky at cards, lucky in love" had better be true or I'll be out all around.

I'm having a difficult time finding words tonight, so perhaps I had better sign off with –

Love and Kisses,

Don

In September, Donald had begun serving on the destroyer USS *Gatling* as an assistant gunnery officer. When he wrote the following letter, the ship was conducting battle exercises off the coast of Bermuda.[2]

This was likely the first message he sent to Mardy after the extended vacation the two spent together before he left the country. For nearly three blissful weeks, they had retreated to the Storey family's cherished vacation home, Checkered Rocks, on a lake in upstate New York. It was probably the longest stretch of time they'd spent together, and they were most likely planning their wedding during the trip, evidenced by Donald's reference to "that big day" in his letter.

[No address information available]

September 13, 1943
Letter #1

Darling –

I am beginning to realize just how grand a time we had during those 19 days. If we ever have another chance like that! How's your dad coming along with his daiquiris? Don't forget a certain little pledge we cooked up. How is mom?

Hope your new job will be what you want. I guess you won't be a working gal for a while yet, and can't say I blame you much.

I would give my last sou* for another week at Checkered Rocks with you, but guess I'd better hang on to my sous and anticipate that big day in the not too distant future – I hope!

Thus far I'm hale and hearty. Hope it lasts! By the way, sweets, how was your chin when I left? I tried to be careful, but I'm like a bull in a china shop sometimes. Now that I think of it, we wasted plenty of time sleeping. Wish I could as I'm having a hard job finding things to say. Perhaps I need a good secretary. A certain Mardy Stickles would fill the bill. Can I offer you a position?

I certainly appreciated every minute spent in the Stickles household and with the Stickles family. I'll do my best to drop your mother and dad a line when I get a chance.

My return address is on the envelope, so start dropping me a few lines. Well darling, I've got to get busy. Love you more than ever.

Always yours,

Don

---

* A coin worth about five cents.[3]

CHAPTER THREE

Marriage

Because so few of Mardy's letters survived the years, the following entries offer some of the only glimpses into her reciprocal love and intense longing for Donald. Mardy's happy-go-lucky writing reveals a little about her personality. Her closing reference to Donald and herself as a "boy" and a "girl" reminds us how very young they were, and how fast they had to grow up.

Mardy's lighthearted prose may also have been intentional, so as not to worry Donald about anything. Her descriptive notes about daily goings–on and the entertainment of the time were sure to keep Donald feeling more connected to home, especially during his loneliest moments.

Mardy mailed the first letter in this chapter when Donald was stationed in Bermuda,[1] a few weeks before the couple's wedding. She was still reveling in the memories of their vacation at the lake house.

Miss Mardy Stickles
Mt. Vernon, N.Y.

Ensign D. E. Storey, U.S.N.
U.S.S. Gatling (D.D.671)
c/o Fleet Post Office
New York, N.Y.

[Postmarked September 28, 1943]
Tuesday
[Letter not dated]

Darling –

No mail today, and I'm really beginning to worry about my letters. I hope by now you've gotten some of them. I don't know what I can do about them, and of course since you haven't gotten them you can't tell me what's wrong. I'll just continue to write them and hope you get them before you get entirely disgusted with me.

Nothing is new, per usual. As you can see by the date, I don't even know what day it is. I can't even remember what I did yesterday except that I read two books.

Today I got out my winter things and took them to the cleaners and started putting my summer things away. Mo* and I went to the movies this afternoon. We saw "Heaven Can Wait" with Don Ameche and Gene Tierney. It was in Technicolor. She really is one of the prettiest girls I've ever seen. The other was one of the Mexican Spitfire series with Lupe Velez and Leon Errol. Horrid, naturally, like most double features.

On the Make Believe Ballroom** Gary Stevens is singing "Yesterday's Gardenias" – that's really a sad song.

Tonight Connie wants to talk, so my next letter will probably contain more news. She will probably know more about you than I do myself. She always does. Well, anyway, I'm grateful for the diversion.

Gary is now singing "White Christmas". I'm so glad they are going to be able to make more records now,*** because all the others I've attached to different things. Most of them to you or to something we did when they were popular. Remember the night you helped me with my Xmas cards, and then got peeved because I did them? We had an awful lot of fun Xmas, even though it was hectic. I can always remember sleeping on your shoulder coming up from N.Y. after work, then having dinner and off again. We did have an awful lot of fun, but I don't think I really knew you until this past 19 days. At least I didn't know a lot of things about you.

I'll find me another book and settle down under the blanket and read and listen to the radio. Right now I'm freezing, so I think it sounds like a good idea.

It will be three weeks tomorrow since I've seen you, darling, and it seems like three years. I don't even think the last two weeks when you were in Florida went as slowly as these past three weeks.

Daddy just drove up, so I guess I'd better get busy and set the table. Daddy and I had a nice little argument last night, and I'm mad. Of course he's forgotten all about it now. He never remembers when I win, but always when he does. Oh well, I don't feel like being mad anymore.

Well darling, I've got to close for today. I miss you so very much, and I hope you'll be coming home real soon.

Don't oversleep, and watch out for your double chin. I'm only kidding — I think you're the most wonderful boy ever, and that I'm the luckiest girl ever.

Yours always,
Mardy

---

*Presumably a friend.

** *The Make Believe Ballroom* was a syndicated radio program hosted by Martin Block. Block played his records from a studio, but made it seem like he was broadcasting from a dance floor.[2]

***Early records were pressed in shellac, but because of the war, shellac, used for making explosives, was in short supply. As a result, new record production was cut down dramatically. To solve the dilemma, record manufacturers turned to vinyl. [3]

This next letter was written just a few weeks after Donald and Mardy's wedding on Wednesday, October 20, 1943, in Mt. Vernon. It was an intimate church ceremony attended by their immediate families. The couple had a small window of time to celebrate, since Donald was in town for only a few days. His ship, the *Gatling*, moored in the Brooklyn Navy Yard from October 17–26, before heading out for Norfolk, Virginia.[4] Mardy met him there for a few days of honeymoon before they had to part again.

In her writing, Mardy grappled with the odd loneliness of being a newly-wed in wartime. She described in detail how she travelled north from Virginia by ship, then on to her parents' house by train. As she tried settling in at home without her husband, she took solace in cataloguing their wedding presents and included a couple of little illustrations for Donald's amusement. Much of her seven-page letter focused on seemingly mundane details, such as scheduling and casual visits with family and friends. It's as if she was trying to recreate every moment of their first days of marriage so Donald could experience them with her. As she wrote on their three-week wedding anniversary, the *Gatling* was en route to Trinidad to escort the aircraft carrier *Langley* to the Delaware Bay.[5]

Mrs. D.E. Storey
Mt. Vernon, N.Y.

Ensign D. E. Storey, U.S.N.
U.S.S. Gatling (D.D. 671)
c/o Fleet Post Office
New York, N.Y.

[Postmarked November 11, 1943]
Wednesday
3rd Anniversary
[Letter not dated]

My Darling –
I shouldn't have to tell you how I felt at 3:45 the morning you left. It gets harder every time to say "goodbye" instead of easier.

Marion* and I had breakfast and then went over to the depot – we were very lucky and got a reservation for the 7:30 boat. We saw Nancy and Phyl off in the morning and Betty off at noon, and then we decided to be reckless and play the slot machines. I lost a dollar – but Marion lost 5 or 6 so I wasn't too bad. We then went upstairs to talk and then had lunch and packed in the afternoon. I got everything in after sitting on my bags – and discovered that you'd left your toothbrush. Do you want me to send it to you, or what? About 6 destroyers came in and we kept hoping one might be yours but after dinner when we hadn't heard from you we knew it was just wishful thinking. We checked out at 7:15 – left forwarding addresses and paid our bill.

We then went down to get the boat and had to wait an hour for it – it was late. We left at 8:30 and had a sandwich and a cup of coffee. You know I've been on the boats that go to Europe or Indies – and of course my ideas of staterooms were as they were when I saw Dotty or Mary** off somewhere. This was so small either Marion or I had to sit on the bunks while the other undressed. I sat first and Marion had the lower so there I tried. I had a terrific time. I was laughing so hard I couldn't do a thing. I kept thinking of your locker episode aboard the Gatling and just laughed even harder.

Jeepers was I lonesome. Do you suppose I'll ever get over that lost feeling when you're not around?

I've collected soap, and now I have soap from the Hotel Lex, Chamberlin, and Old Bayline. We'll have plenty of that if it doesn't get funny by then – or whatever it does. We got off at 8:30 and just made the 8:45 for New York – and then just made the 12:55 for Mr. Vernon. Mom was having "the girls" for lunch – so we joined them and then gabbed all day. Marion didn't feel like dinner so she retired and mommy, daddy, Judy*** and I went out for dinner. Then I went to bed at 10:30 and slept 'till 11:30 this morning. I got up and put on your robe and decided that I'd better get myself a warm robe and give yours back to you before I wear it out entirely.

It's so cold here I nearly froze – that was the beginning of the freeze, and tonight I'm only going to open one window. We had breakfast, talked, then lunch, and then Daddy took us all to Pelham to see them play Pleasantville. Georgie and Don and Gilly are all on the team so we really enjoyed ourselves. I saw Harriet, Bobby, Mr. L. and Uncle Earl, and of course that was the first time I'd seen any of them since I became Mrs. Donald E. Storey. I was just proud as punch – everyone thinks I'm the luckiest person alive and so do I. Our feet were frozen, and we came home and had a hi-ball, and Dad said to be sure to tell you that he had a coffee royal for you. We are just beginning to thaw out now and are getting ready for dinner.

We had quite a few wedding presents waiting for us when I got home. A darling sterling silver nut dish from Tiffany's from your step grandmother – 8 cocktail glasses from Miles and Lucille [drawing] all different colors. Two darling pictures from Julie. A huge mirror in a gold frame that will look gorgeous over a fireplace from Gene and Virginia – two hurricane lamps from Mrs. B. – with a sterling silver candle stick like this [drawing]. I'm an awful artist but you can get the general idea. And a beautiful set of china from Mr. and Mrs. W., and a 25 dollar check from George G. with a very sweet note. The check I'm depositing with the one you gave me – so we did rather well. We have 3 parcel slips to pick up at the post office so I'll probably have more to write you tomorrow.

Darling I'd give anything if you could be home with me to open them – but I'll get a thrill all over again when I show them to you next time you're in.

You know – I'm so very glad we had the time we had in Virginia – I had such a marvelous time. I always do when I'm with you, but it's so much nicer to have you almost like a business man and come home at night. The times I've spent with you since Oct. 20th has been the happiest time of my life. I'll bet there isn't another person in the whole world that has ever been as happy as I am. I guess you can rather imagine from this letter that I'm a little in love with you and I hope you don't mind.

I got your letter when you (excuse) I got home and it was wonderful. I've read it six times already and the edges are so very worn. Did you get my nic-nac?

Well, darling – I've got to eat and then I'm going to call <u>our</u> folks – and besides if I don't stop soon I won't be able to get this in the envelope.

I love you with all my heart.

Mardy

P.S. Hurry home!

P.S.S. I love you

P.S.S.S. XXXXOOOO C.O.D.

---

*All the people named in this letter were friends, unless otherwise noted.

**Dotty and Mary were aunts on Mardy's mother's side.

***Judy was Mardy's sister. She died a couple of years before Mardy.

Donald and Mardy were briefly reunited during Thanksgiving week, because the *Gatling* was in Norfolk, Virginia. Just a month into their marriage, Mardy was feeling grateful for, though unfulfilled by, these temporary visits. On the morning of November 25, Thanksgiving Day, Mardy saw Donald off again, and penned this letter over the weekend. By November 30, the ship was back in Norfolk for a few days before setting off for the Panama Canal.[6]

Mrs. D.E. Storey
Mt. Vernon, N.Y.

Ensign D. E. Storey, U.S.N.
U.S.S. Gatling (D.D. 671)
c/o Fleet Post Office
New York, N.Y.

[Postmarked November 29, 1943]
Sunday
[Letter not dated]

My dearest –

I miss you so very much. All day I've had a feeling that you might call either to talk or that you were in somewhere and now it's time to call it another day and no word. I know I'm silly after all you said but I just can't help feeling this way.

Nothing much is new since yesterday. Your wife got feeling rather high last night, under the influence of Mary, Jack, Eddie,* Mom and Dad. We got a floor lamp from Aunt Eddie, and a carving set (it's a beauty) from Uncle Jack.

Today I went to church per usual, then Eddie and Sue** came over and we had daiquiris. I'm now off them and liquor until next weekend. You know, it just isn't any fun doing anything without you. This aft. Judy and I went to the movies and saw "Wintertime" with Sonja Henie. It was very good, and another picture that was sad as the dickens and of course I wept buckets. Aren't you glad you weren't there.

Tomorrow is wash day so I'll tackle my things and yours and in the afternoon mother and I are going to get Xmas cards and figure out who we are going to give presents to this year.

Well, darling, tomorrow I'll have more to say and I hope I have a letter soon. Goodness – I saw you Thursday morning – it isn't even a week since I saw you last and I feel like it's been the longest time ever.

Everyone sends their love and kisses, me too especially.

Forever Yours,

Mardy

---

*Extended family members. "Eddie" was the nickname given to Mardy's Aunt Edna.

**Sue was Edna's daughter.

CHAPTER FOUR

Separated at Christmas

Christmas had to be the loneliest time for service members, away from their families and loved ones. Writing, at least, seemed to provide some solace from the emptiness they undoubtedly felt during a traditional time of family togetherness.

As Donald traveled from the Panama Canal to San Francisco and on to Hawaii, his feelings of isolation grew. To cope, he sent a flurry of letters to his new bride. They disclose a range of emotions: boredom, anxiety, exhaustion, anticipation, and of course, love.

During this period, Donald numbered some of his letters—perhaps anticipating the disorganized holiday mail delivery—but much of the correspondence from this grouping seems to have been lost.

When Donald wrote the first letter presented in this chapter, the *Gatling* was moored at Balboa Harbor in the Pacific Ocean, after escorting the USS *Intrepid* aircraft carrier to and through the Panama Canal. The next day, they would start out for San Francisco.[1]

Ens. DE Storey, USN
USS Gatling
c/o F.P.O. N.Y.

Mrs. D. E. Storey
Mt. Vernon
N.Y.

Monday
December 13, 1943

My Dearest Darling –

Hello precious, here's your lonesome loving husband once again. Gosh, it is only 12 days until Santa comes and I keep getting farther and farther away. Now, just what is the sense in that?

We've been sitting here twiddling our thumbs for the past few days, but expect we'll be moving soon. Perhaps I'll have a chance to call you around Xmas day. Not sure as yet, however.

The officers are supposed to play the chiefs in baseball this afternoon, but I have the duty so guess I'll have to stay out of the fun. Personally, I don't care about going. I'd rather settle down with you and watch the rest of the world pass by.

I saw "Blood and Sand"* last night. An old picture, the second time I've seen it, but it was still enjoyable. I'm anxious to get some of your letters and hear all the news from home. Just talked to Al** and since they need a good man on first base I'm getting to get some exercise – which I need. I'll be fat and flabby if I don't get some now and then. Don't you say a word!

Sweets, I don't know how you feel but I've already passed the stage where I miss you. Now I'm at the point where my soul aim in life and all my thoughts center on how soon I can come back to you, to our home (to be), etc.!!!

Precious, I've got work to do per usual, and I'm running out of ink and stationary so I'll say goodbye.

I'll Love You Forever,

Don

P.S. Give my love to all. I love you, my darling, with all my heart.

Me

---

*A 1941 romantic drama starring Tyrone Power, Linda Darnell, and Rita Hayworth.[2]

**Unless otherwise noted, the men Donald references in his letters are presumed to be crewmates.

By the time Donald wrote this next letter, he had been at sea for several days, en route to San Francisco. The realities of life on board a destroyer were settling in, and Donald was growing weary. Memories of the last time he and Mardy parted didn't help his mood. Neither did his wishes to be back at the Naval Academy, just so he could be with his new bride. To cope, he relied on the possibility of a phone call and hoped for better Christmases to come.

Ens. DE Storey, USN
USS Gatling
c/o Fleet Post Office
San Francisco, Cal.

Mrs. D. E. Storey
Mt. Vernon
New York

Saturday
Dec. 18, 1943
7

My Dearest Darling,

Hello again, beautiful. I haven't written for the past two days, but have really been quite busy and very, very tired from the mid watch which means four hours sleep a night. I could stand about 48 hours of good solid sleep. However, I'd forego all sleep if it would mean seeing you. It seems like such a long time since that black morning I waved goodby to you in the window.

We had a humdinger of a rough night the night before last. My Christmas presents were stowed on top of my locker, but before the night was over they were all over the deck after having hit various people in the eye in the course of their flight. I gathered them all together again and put them back where they will remain until a week from today. I didn't get sick, so guess I'm finally turning into an old salt. However, it was not a very comfortable night.

I enjoyed our short stay in Panama. It is a very colorful place, but I wouldn't want to stay there over a week or so. The towers at both ends of the canal are filled with curio shops and honky tonks. I'd like very much to turn around and go through again – West to East – without stopping.

Darling, in some ways I wish I were back at USNA if I could be there and be married to you at the same time. What I mean is that I'm jealous as I know they are just about to start on a two week vacation. However, all things considered I'm darn glad to be out.

Hope I'll have a chance to call you around Christmas day, but if I don't I want you to know that I will be with you in spirit and in love. Next year I intend to be with you in person – by fair means or foul.

Angel, that's about all there is for now. I love you with all my heart and think and dream of you both night and day.

I'll Love You Forever,

Don

XXXXX – For Xmas!

With four days to go until Christmas, Donald was still counting the weeks since he last saw his wife, and projected himself into Mardy's life by imagining what she was doing back home. As the *Gatling* neared San Francisco, he was eager to be in port so he could attempt a call—a fleeting antidote to his sense of separation.

Ens. DE Storey, USN
USS Gatling
c/o Fleet Post Office
San Francisco, Cal.

Mrs. D. E. Storey
Mt. Vernon
N.Y.

Tuesday
Dec. 21, 1943
9

My Darling –
Three weeks ago tonight was our last night together.* It seems like much more than that now. It should be at least three months! I wonder what you are doing tonight. It probably is cold out and right now you are finishing supper (with cocktail before) and are feeling very chipper. I'm sitting here waiting for the evil hour of 7:45 to roll around when I must go on watch, but my mind is far off with a little "buggy" that I love.

Weather took a turn towards the colder side today but it feels pretty good for a change. Expect to be in port soon and I do hope I can get a call through. The lines are undoubtedly very busy at this season of the year, so you will probably be awakened at an ungodly hour if I can get one through.

Afraid this letter will really have to be cut short as I have to run and relieve the watch. I love you passionately with all my heart and I miss everything about you.

Forever Yours,

Don

---

*He may have been mistaken about the date. The last time the couple met up was on Thanksgiving, which was about four weeks before this letter.

When the USS *Gatling* arrived in San Francisco, Donald wrote Mardy a letter from his room that night on hotel stationery. He didn't stay in town long; the next day his ship was en route to Pearl Harbor.[3]

Hotel Sir Francis Drake
San Francisco

Mrs. D.E. Storey
Mt. Vernon
New York

Wednesday
Dec. 22, 1943
10

My Darling –
Right now, I am sitting here waiting to get a call through to you, with two rye and ginger ales by my side. Angel, I miss you so much tonight that I am sorely tempted to call it quits. We could hide away at "Checkered Rocks" until after the shooting match is over. However, something inside just won't let me do that. I know you wouldn't let me either.

Four of us have a room here for the night – also a bottle – so I guess we will proceed to get politely stinko. May be the last one for a long while. I can't seem to appreciate tonight, however, when I realize that you are in the U.S., I am in the U.S., and we are 4000 miles apart. Especially so now that Christmas is but three days off.

Jake tells me that you, Phyllis and Mildred* had a get together yesterday. I would have liked to have bought all three of you a drink and then whisked you off where you and I could be together alone for a long, long time.

Right now Bing is singing "I'll be Home for Xmas" – wish to God that were true. I'd give most anything – except you – to walk into the Stickles house in Mt. Vernon on Dec. 24th and take you into my arms.

We had a fairly nice trip – good weather at least. Thus far I have seen very little of Frisco and doubt if I will get a chance to see much. Seems like a nice place from what little I have seen.

Expect to get some letters from you tomorrow. Can't wait to hear all the dope from the home front.

Sweets, I'm going to sign off now. Love you with all my heart and wish you were here beside me.

Forever Yours,

Don

---

*Unidentified people; probably friends.

Donald's longing to be with Mardy leading up to the holiday reached its peak in his Christmas Day message. It is this letter that confirms the couple became engaged exactly one year earlier. The uncertainty of wartime seems to have sped up life's landmark moments.

It appears Santa was good to Donald. He received lots of gifts, and a bundle of Mardy's letters in time for the holiday. He was even able to get a call through to her. But a statement near the end of this message revealed the possibility of the biggest gift of all. Could Mardy have been pregnant?

Ens. DE Storey, USN
USS Gatling
c/o Fleet Post Office
San Francisco, Cal.

Mrs. D.E. Storey
Mt. Vernon
New York

Saturday
Dec. 25, 1943
Christmas!!
11

My Dearest Darling –
As my pen writes the following words it will not do justice to the loneliness that has been in my heart all day. If I ever hear any suggestion of being away from you at Christmas time again! I had a very nice Christmas, under the existing circumstances, but there was a great deal to be desired. When I realize that a year ago tonight was our first night as an engaged couple! What a lemon I was on that night! If I had to do it all over again, however, I don't believe I'd change a thing. I have a host of memories – all of them good. Do you remember two years ago when Al made a nuisance of himself – in my opinion? Yes, my beautiful wife, you made me very jealous. Was I obstreperous that night? I can't recall.

I love you, darling, and I love each and every one of my Christmas presents from the spear-o-mint life savers to the leather jacket waiting at home. Those cuff links are grand. Mother and Dad gave me a nice wallet, collar box, and a razor. All in all, I had a plentiful Christmas. We had a tremendous dinner and the Red Cross gave every man and officer presents which consisted of small bags containing books, playing cards, soap, cigarettes, etc. Even had a Santa Claus!!

Darling, I received your letters and they were more than welcome. Also heard from Ev, "Gran", Mother, and Dad. I certainly appreciate mail – even more than I did at USNA. Your letters get sweeter and better all the time. Wish I could write as good a letter.

I enjoyed talking to you so very much the other night and for once in my life I didn't want to put the phone down. You sounded so sleepy, lonesome, and scrumptious that I wanted to become an electron and flow from minus to plus – Frisco to New York. I had quite a job getting the call through, but if I hadn't talked to you I would have been a blue "buggy".

On the watch today, we fixed up the phone circuits so that all the guns and stations were beaming music from the radio shack. We also had a Christmas program this evening at which there were short skits, carols, and a bit of religion. All in all, Christmas was celebrated as best we could and still keep the USS Gatling afloat and in motion.

Hey Angel, I'm going to retire! You'll be making enough money for the both of us! How did you happen to fall into the job? Sounds wonderful and I do hope you like it. Every time I hear "The Blue Network"* now I can say "There's my snookie". Hope your boss is fat, bald, and fortyish!!

Darling, I won't say too much about my second reason for celebrating the other night, but if it's true, I'm all for it. Will say no more 'till I hear from you.

Darling, there is so much I can write but I think I'll save it for future letters. I love you so very very much, dearest, and have been with you all day. My very best to Gram, Dad and Judy.

Forever Yours,

Don

P.S. I'd love some wristlets!!

---

*It is not known how long Mardy worked as a secretary for The Blue Network, a conglomerate of radio stations that was rebranded as ABC in 1945 before pivoting to TV a few years later. [4]

Donald wrote the following letter a day before the *Gatling* arrived in Pearl Harbor. He was still feeling the effects of being away from Mardy on such an important holiday.

Ens. DE Storey, USN
USS Gatling
c/o Fleet Post Office
San Francisco, Calif.

Mrs. D.E. Storey
Mt. Vernon
New York

Monday
Dec. 27, 1943
12

My Darling –
Good evening, angel, and how are you feeling tonight? Expect you have returned from your first day at the office. How did it feel to ride the commuter's special once again? Sometimes I wish I were riding it in your place – in fact nearly all the time.

Expect to be putting in someplace where I can mail this tomorrow. Wish it were New York where I could play postman and bring my letters in person.

Remember that false alarm about Fred Waring* and our song? Well, in about five or six weeks we're expecting him to dedicate a program to the "Rattlin Battlin Gatlin",** so start listening in a month or so. Probably a false alarm again!

I've been sort of down in the dumps today for no good reason. Reckon it must be the aftermath of Christmas. I missed you so much Saturday, darling, because there were so many memories brought home throughout the day. I practically lived Christmas Day with you from midnight mass 'til hamburgers at the Westchester Grill. It was such a busy day that I guess I haven't fully recovered yet.

This trip has been fairly easy on the constitution as we have three passengers which means less watches. As a matter of fact, I had ten solid hours of sleep last night which is unheard of under our normal organization.

Darling, you told me to ask for things when I need 'em. Well, I'd like air mail stamps – about $5 worth as they are precious as gold out here.

I love you, my dearest, and want nothing more than to spend the rest of my life by your side.

Forever yours,

Don

XOXOX – Happy New Year!

---

*Fredrick Waring was a musician, composer, choral conductor, bandleader, and preeminent music educator.[5]

**"The Rattlin' Battlin' Gatling" was the name of the ship's song.[6]

CHAPTER FIVE

Hawaii

The USS *Gatling* remained in Pearl Harbor for the first half of January, 1944.[1] The naval base had recovered from the 1941 Japanese attack,[2] but Hawaii was still under martial law.[3]

Amid the beauty of the Pacific, Donald and the rest of the destroyer's crew were gearing up for battle by conducting tactical maneuvers, anti-submarine warfare training, radar and gunnery exercises, and flight operations.[4] But they also found time for some rest. Donald enjoyed the beaches and night life available to him when he could—a respite, perhaps, for the constant questions that lingered in his head—among them, was he going to be a father? Cut off from any communication with Mardy, he would have to wait indefinitely to find out.

Ens. DE Storey, USN
USS Gatling (DD 671)
c/o Fleet Post Office
San Francisco, Cal.

Mrs. D.E. Storey
Mt. Vernon
New York

Sunday
Jan. 2, 1944
14

My Dearest Darling –
Another couple of days nearer to the time when we will be together again.
By the way, "Happy New Year". I went swimming on the afternoon of
New Year's Eve at that famous beach* but was back on board by 6:30.
Dropped in at the officers club for a few drinks and bumped into King,
Moose S., and John S. – also Bill H. Guess you'd meet most anyone – in
the naval line – if you stick around here long enough.

Darling, I've been looking forward so much to hearing from you ever
since we left Frisco but thus far no luck. Perhaps my ship will come in
soon.

I've missed you something dreadful lately. I've been away far too long
already, but there doesn't seem to be any prospect of coming home for a
long, long while so I guess we'll have to "grin and bear it" – well, "bear it"
anyhow. Gets mighty hard sometimes, but when I get sort of low I just remember what a wonderful wife I have waiting for me and my spirits jump
right up – the little devils.

Darling, I wish there were a new and different way to say I love you.
Perhaps if I weren't me, I'd find a way, but being as I is me I'll close for
tonight by saying – I love you, my darling.

And will Forever,

Don

XOX

---

*Donald was most likely referring to Waikiki Beach.

Cut off from his old life and half a world away from his wife, Donald started to imagine impossible reunion scenarios. The separation was enough to test anyone's nerves. With circumstances so out of his control, it's no wonder Donald thought he might be losing his mind.

Ens. DE Storey, USN
USS Gatling (DD 671)
c/o Fleet Post Office
San Francisco, Cal.

Mrs. D.E. Storey
Mt. Vernon
New York

Wednesday
January 5th, 1944
16

My Dearest Darling –
Another day – another dollar. I'm a tired person tonight. Not used to so much leg exercise, or perhaps I'm getting to be an old man. Just returned from the movies. Saw a good picture tonight entitled "Watch on the Rhine"* – very deep but good.

Darling, have you ever slept under mosquito netting? It's the damndest stuff. I woke up last night about one o'clock and had to take a short journey. Forgetting where I was and being half asleep I just sort of jumped up. I ended up on the floor ensnarled in yards of mosquito netting. I sat there and laughed because I thought how much you would have enjoyed it all – stinker.

Angel, the nights are so beautiful out here that it seems a shame to waste them. C'mon out and stay with me for a while. I sure would love to kiss you just once – in a while. Do my letters sound to you as if I am slowly getting a bit unsound in the mind? Reading them over, I sometimes wonder. Darling, I love you – even if I am going slightly mad – mad at the world for keeping you so far from me.

Snooks, I'm going to beg off and hit the hay. Love you, adorable, and miss you now and then – in a pig's ear – it's now and always.

Forever Yours,

Donnie

---

*A 1943 movie with Bette Davis and Paul Lukas, who won an Academy Award for his role. [5]

In this letter, Donald revealed he was off the ship in training. Still awaiting news from Mardy, he looked forward to her upcoming birthday and reminisced about their early movie dates when their love was blossoming.

Ens. DE Storey, USN
USS Gatling (DD 671)
c/o Fleet Post Office
San Francisco, Cal.

Mrs. D.E. Storey
Mt. Vernon
N.Y.

Jan. 6th, 1944
Thursday
17

Dearest Darling –
Here I be at the end of another day. This sure is a nice healthy life. Nine hours of sleep a night, a long day of work, the movies, a beer or two and then to bed. I'll be sorry to see it end. I really look like I've been working anyhow as I get full of grease, oil, etc.

Perhaps you've gathered by now that I'm at a gunnery school. Don't know why I didn't tell you in the two previous letters, but don't guess the censor will object as I can't mail these 'til I'm back aboard anywho.

How are you darling. Haven't heard from you since our telephone call, and that sure seems like a heck of a long time ago. Sure will be glad to hear about your job and other things!

Darling, is there anything special you'd like for your birthday? I'd give a million to be able to take you out dancing that day. What am I talking about? Perhaps some miracle will happen – it will take just that – and I will be able to take my beloved out. Besides it's a month away and plenty can happen in a month – I've found that out in this past one.

Saw another movie tonight called "City for Conquest".* I'd seen it about a year ago, but enjoyed it for the second time. We have had lots of movie dates, angel. I remember so well when we used to go in the afternoons during my summer leaves. I used to think I loved you then, but I didn't know what it is to be in love. I must have been infatuated, but, thank goodness, the infatuation readily gave way to the greatest sensation and feeling anyone could ask for – to love with the sweetest "snookie" in the whole wide world – believe you me it is wide, too!

Angel, before I say goodnight let me say just this – I love you and I will never let you out of my sight when this mess is over.

Forever yours,

Donnie

XOX

P.S. Please give my love to Gram, Dad and Judets.**

---

*The 1940 film *City for Conquest* is a love story with its main characters played by James Cagney and Ann Sheridan.[6]

**Donald's nickname for Mardy's sister.

Consumed with lovesickness, Donald dispensed with news of his day-to-day activities in this letter and focused solely on Mardy. Consoled by his only photo of her, he imagined some shenanigans she might get into while he was away, and lightheartedly tried to assert his disapproval. Donald closed his message by fondly recalling their brief honeymoon.

Ens. DE Storey, USN
USS Gatling (DD 671)
c/o Fleet Post Office
San Francisco, Cal.

Mrs. D.E. Storey
Mt. Vernon
N.Y.

Friday
January 7th, 1944

My Dearest Darling –
Just finished a bout of night firing. The effects were pretty – sort of like the 4th of July.

I don't know why but I missed you more today than usual. I kept pulling out my <u>one</u> snapshot of you and just staring with wonder at my gorgeous wife. I had that little piece of mistletoe right along with you in my wallet. You know, darling, I believe I've told you this before but you do have the devil in your eyes. You look like you are up to some sort of mischief – better not be!!

I'm enclosing a picture I saw in the paper this morning.* Look at it closely and then think where and when you have seen its subjects before. If you don't know I'm going to – well, anywho, you'd better remember. I remember so darn well that it hurts. We had such a short time that it could not truly be called a honeymoon – but snooks, it was wonderful – short or no.

Angel, I'm at a loss for words tonight. Sorry – I'll try to do better to-morrow. I love you so very much, sweets – so much that I think I'm gonna bust.

Forever and Ever,

Donnie

---

*This newspaper clipping was missing from the letter.

On January 9, Donald received a parcel of mail from Mardy, who had just taken a new job at Texaco as a stenographer. Her letters seemed to lift him up and take his mind off his melancholy. Only one piece of news was missing: whether or not Mardy was pregnant. Poor Donald would have to wait some more.

Ens. DE Storey, USN
USS Gatling (DD 671)
c/o Fleet Post Office
San Francisco, Cal.

Mrs. D.E. Storey
Mt. Vernon
N.Y.

Sunday
Jan. 9, 1944
19

My Dearest –
I hope 19 is the right number, but I've forgotten although I know it is somewhere around there. A wonderful thing happened today – I received mail. They were considerate enough to forward my letters to me, and I sure was glad to hear from you. I'm so glad to hear that you had a good Christmas. We certainly have received plenty of presents, and I'm living for the day when we can begin to put them to good use.

Mother and Dad certainly loved having you with them and are nuts about my wife – can't understand it!! Darling, anybody that is not crazy about you is not in his or her right mind. I'm not crazy about you, I just love you, adore you, and want right now to hold you tight and tell you I love you over and over again.

I went "in" today, and "the R.B.G"* has sailed away. I spent about two hours tramping around looking for Skeet** as I heard his craft was in, but I never did find him. Ernst led the duty – so I wandered off to a football game! I saw the Rainbows (Hawaiian All Stars) beat the 7th Army Air

Force. Pretty good game and being my one and only this year I enjoyed it. I'm now back to "school" preparing to start another week.

In some ways I'm glad you are working – mainly because it gives you something to do. However, resign as soon as you feel like resigning. I'm jealous of the boss – stinker that I am – because he gets to see you every day. I'd pay lots more than $32.50 a week for that privilege.

Darling, I'm still in the dark as to whether we are to be "three". Your letters, coming all together, do not straighten me out very well. "Yes" or "no" is great with me, so how about giving it to me right from the shoulder.

I'm going to have quite a bunch of letters to mail when I do finally get the chance. Angel, in each and every one I tell you that I love you and in each and every one I mean it from the bottom of my heart. I'd better quit before "I" start feeling sorry for me.

I Love You,
Donnie

---

*Rattlin' Battlin' Gatling.

**Presumably a friend and classmate from the Naval Academy.

In the middle of writing the following letter, Donald was called away and didn't return to finish it until four days later. The distraction may have been a precursor for what lay ahead; as Donald warned Mardy she might not hear from him for a while.

Ens. DE Storey, USN
USS Gatling (DD 671)
c/o Fleet Post Office
San Francisco, Cal.

Mrs. D.E. Storey
Mt. Vernon
N.Y.

Monday
Jan. 10th, 1944
20

My Dearest Darling –
Another week under way. Darling, I think that our Christmas card was very "chique" or something to that effect. "Mardy and Don Storey" – that sounds wonderful and is wonderful. I read all your letters over again today and they are scrumptious. You are a mighty wonderful wife, and I love you a little bit – a little bit more than I did yesterday.

In the paper today I read something about Billy R. playing on some basketball team. Seems funny to hear about people you used to know when you're so far from home. I'd much rather be reading it in the Daily Argus.*

Friday
Jan. 14th, 1944

Hello angel! I was interrupted right in the midst of my literary efforts, but here I am again – back aboard the "R.B.G." They cut my course short just when I was catching up on my sleep. However, there was a grand letter waiting for me when I got back so I wasn't mad.

Darling, if the time comes when you don't hear from me for a long while, please don't worry. It'll just be that I won't have the opportunity to write any letters. I've been trying to be good about writing, and don't think I've done too bad a job.

How's the work coming along? Hope you like it, but if you don't please don't hesitate to throw in the towel. I want you to do whatever you want to, as your happiness means more to me than anything else. Hope this war hurries up and peters out. I've had a plenty already and would be mighty content to be Mr. John Civilian with a rose covered 2 x 4, a fireplace, and you – most of all.

Stan** tells me you gals didn't even get tipsy New Year's Eve. What's the matter "rummy" have you lost the knack? I'll be only too glad to show you how again – although I'm not much of an expert – especially with champagne if you'll remember rightly.

Darling, I often wonder what things would be like if I hadn't been persistent and kept dogging your steps. To me you are every sweet, loveable, and wonderful thing all rolled into one bundle.

Forever Yours,

Don

P.S. Give the folks my love.

---

* Mount Vernon's local newspaper at the time.[7]

**Another friend.

Donald wrote this next letter shortly before heading out toward his first battle. On January 16, 1944, The *Gatling* joined the destroyers, aircraft carriers, oilers, and cruisers of Task Group 58.1 and left Pearl Harbor to assist in the planned invasion of the Japanese-occupied Marshall Islands in the central Pacific.[8] Donald didn't mention a word of this, however. His message was casual and filled with his usual warmth.

Ens. DE Storey, USN
USS Gatling (DD 671)
c/o Fleet Post Office
San Francisco, Cal.

Mrs. D.E. Storey
Mt. Vernon
N.Y.

Saturday
Jan. 15th, 1944
21

My Dearest Darling –
Hi beautiful! 'Tis early in the morn, but I can do nothing but think of you. We had a mail delivery yesterday but not a letter did I receive – it was all non-airmail and was at least a month old. I went ashore for an hour and a half yesterday and acquired a slight glow.

Darling, this will probably be the last letter for quite some time, so don't worry when you don't get any mail. I'll still be thinking of you and loving you much as ever.

I got shot yesterday – with tetanus toxoid and my arm feels like a lump of lead. However, if it could hold you I know darn well it would rise to the occasion. Sometimes I certainly feel as if my letters are nuts. The major issue is, however, that I love you and want you with all my heart.

Perhaps I've said enough for now. Take care of yourself, darling, and remember that I'm always with you in spirit.

Forever Yours,

Donnie

CHAPTER SIX

Mardy's News and the Marshall Islands

As Donald wrote to Mardy on the eve of leaving for the invasion of the Marshall Islands, Mardy composed a note that would change his life. She was pregnant—just as Donald had suspected! Though he probably didn't receive the letter for weeks, it illuminated the two worlds they occupied: his of death and destruction; hers with the promise of new life.

The following letter is the one I read at Mardy's internment service nearly seventy-four years later.

Mrs. D.E. Storey
Mt. Vernon, New York

Ensign D.E. Storey, U.S.N.
U.S.S. Gatling (D.D. 671)
c/o Fleet Post Office
San Francisco, Calif.

Saturday
January 15, 1944

My Dearest Darling –

I guess the best way to start this letter is to tell the news. I went to Dr. Bell this morning and come the end of August or the beginning of September you are going to be a father and I am going to be a mother. I can't help being excited and just thrilled to death and I hope you won't be too disappointed. I'm an awfully healthy person and can work until May or the beginning of June.

I told Dad and Judy when I got home, and they are delighted. Dad is sure it's going to be a boy because he's always wanted a football player. Everyone – especially me – wants it to look just like you. Nothing more is new in that line, and I'll keep you posted I promise – but please don't worry. Honestly, I'm so darn happy I could split. I'm going to tell Didi and Dad* when they come down – but I'm not going to tell anyone else in my family or anything because I want it to be a surprise, I want to keep working, and I sort of hope maybe perhaps you might get home sometime between now and Sept.

I got my first check the other day – enclosed is the stub** – pretty nice isn't it. Of course that's for 14 days – but it still looks good to me. I put $66.00 in the bank – $10.00 toward a War Bond – and $5.00 I owed Dad and the rest to buy my lunches. The first of February we'll have approximately $600.00 in the bank – maybe more. Isn't that neat!

Last night Judy and I went to see "Phantom of the Opera", and it was grand – then we had a soda and came home. Tonight Dad, Mom and I are going to Aunt Eddies and then out for dinner and Judy's going to a dance. That about covers my weekend activities outside of missing you and wishing you were here.

I haven't heard from you this week so I called Connie to see if Ev had said anything, he thinks you're in gunnery school and I certainly hope so. Honestly, darling, I hate having you away from me, but I dread the thought of you in danger.

Well, my darling, I'm not very good at writing this letter, but I'm not so sure of your reaction! I know it's much sooner than you expected – but it's happened anyway.

I love you with all my heart.

Mardy

P.S. Enclosed the stamps you wanted – please ask me for whatever you want!

XXXXX

OOOOO

Me

---

*Donald's parents.

**Mardy's pay stub, enclosed with her letter, was issued by The Texas Company (Texaco) and dated January 13, 1944. Her earnings of $88.44 had a federal insurance contribution of 88 cents and federal withholding tax of $3.60. The amount she had left for her lunches was $2.96.

Saturday
January 15, 1944

My dearest darling -

I guess the best way to start this letter is to tell the news. I went to Dr. Bell this morning and come the end of august or the beginning of September you are going to be a father and I am going to be a mother. I can't help being excited and just thrilled to death and I hope you won't be too disappointed. I'm an awfully healthy person and can work until May or the beginning of June.

I know it's much sooner than you expected - but it's happened anyway -

I love you with all my heart.
Mandy

P.S. Enclosed the stamps you wanted - please ask me for whatever you want!

XXXXX
OOOOO
M.

Unaware of Mardy's news, Donald sat down to write the following letter, as the *Gatling* was in waters off the Marshall Islands.[1] It would be a matter of days before U.S. carrier task forces would launch strikes against Japanese airfields there. Donald didn't let on about the impending attack, except to slyly suggest of some upcoming "fun" and that Mardy should keep up with news from the Pacific.

Ens. DE Storey, USN
USS Gatling (DD 671)
c/o Fleet Post Office
San Francisco, Calif.

Mrs. D.E. Storey
Mt. Vernon
N.Y.

Jan. 25th, 1944
Tuesday
22

My Dearest Darling –
Hi there Mardets! Has been a long time since I last wrote, and will undoubtedly be much longer before this and the letters to follow get mailed. What a relief it will be to have this war over with so there will be no long absences and no long lapse between letters. As I sit here and think of the past and the future everything seems wonderful. The present, however, is not anything to write home about. There is a lot to write home about, but it will all be in the papers soon.

Darling, I lie awake at night dreaming of the days when I won't have to write home. I'll never leave you for a moment if I can get clear of this rumpus and the navy. However, I'm sadly afraid that it will be a long while before I see you again.

I love you, Darling, I can't even tell you how much I mean those words. You are my life, and without you there would be nothing left to keep me going.

I am now a "shellback"* after a various assortment of punishments which took place when we crossed the equator. They had Bud C. and myself up on the focsle** in our undershorts, with no shoes on, acting as lookouts with coke bottles for binoculars. Then they whipped us a bit, introduced us to King Neptune, cut our hair and gave us a shampoo of graphite and fuel oil. More fun!! This all took place a couple of days ago.*** We will be having some more fun in a few days – of a very different nature.

Enough about your errant husband. How are you faring as a hard working young "navy" wife? Don't let your boss fall too hard. If he does I'll just have to punch him in the schnoozz and take my lover away from his stinking old office. Been doing much lately, sweets? I've been doing lots of thinking. Gosh, darling, sometimes it is torture to love anyone as much as I love you. I plot, scheme, and plan all day long with one aim in view – to get home to you and to stay there. Enough for tonight before.I get morbid. My love to all.

I Love You and Worship You,

Don

XOXXXXOX

---

*A Navy sailor becomes a shellback on his first trip across the Equator, during which his crewmates hold an initiation ceremony where attendants pull pranks and dress up as King Neptune and other mythical characters.[2]

**The "forward part of the upper deck of a ship." [3]

***The *Gatling's* log notes the ship crossed the Equator on January 22 at 1300 and "were boarded by Neptunis Rex and his Royal Party." [4]

U.S. aircraft carriers launched planes for a strike on Taroa Island at Maloelap Atoll at sunrise on January 29. Several planes crashed on take-off due to rain, and the *Gatling*'s crew was immersed in rescuing downed crew members. The battle to occupy the Marshall Islands continued with the bombing of Kwajalein Island on January 30 and 31.[5]

Despite this chaos, Donald was able to find the time to write this letter. They could very well have been his only moments of peace. Once again, he could only hint at what was transpiring.

This letter joined others Donald wrote, but was unable to send, until days later.

Ens. DE Storey, USN
USS Gatling (DD 671)
c/o Fleet Post Office
San Francisco, Cal.

Mrs. D.E. Storey
Mt. Vernon
N.Y.

Monday
Jan. 31st, 1944
23

My Dearest Darling –
It has really been a long time between letters this time, snooks, but I know that someday when I can tell you why you will understand. Anyhow, it will be quite some while before any letters fall into the hands of a post man, so by that time I'll have a sizely pack to send if all goes well.

Angel, I could write pages on how much I've missed you the last few weeks. You have been in my thoughts constantly and I try to imagine what you are doing each and every moment of the day.

I have so much to tell you when I see you, but will probably have volumes before that beautiful day arrives. Keep your eye on the paper and you will understand what I am talking about.

The days have been very long lately, and I am in an extremely receptive frame of mind for twelve straight hours of sleep, all of which is out of the question for many a moon. Hope this doesn't sound like I'm complaining, as I really feel grand and seem to get fatter every day. I watch carefully in the mirror to see if I am getting a double chin, but thus far one has not appeared – thank God – except for the "imaginary" one you always claim to see!

If everything goes as well as it has lately, perhaps the war will be over sooner than expected. I pray every night that the damn mess will "bear a hand" so I can come home and we can establish our home. Seems a shame for all those wedding presents to be lying around collecting dust when I want so much to put them to good use.

Enough about the "better half"!! How are you, snooks? I can hardly realize that my little gal will be 21 in a very few days. I'd better hurry up and age a little so you won't disown me for being too young. How do you like Texaco? Suppose we'll have to use that and nothing else in our car.

Darling, I love you so darn much that most of the time I don't know whether I'm coming or going. In spite of being thousands of miles away I'm more sure of my love every minute and I thank the provinces for having given me the good fortune to have the most wonderful wife in the world. My love to Gram, Dad and Judy.

I love you, sweets.

Donnie

XOXX

On the day Donald wrote the following letter, U.S. forces landed on Kwajalein, Roy and Namur Islands, sites of Japanese airfields.[6] The *Gatling* was delegated to search for survivors in the water after two battleships in her task group collided.[7]

Ens. DE Storey, USN
USS Gatling (DD 671)
c/o Fleet Post Office
San Francisco, Cal.

Mrs. D.E. Storey
Mt. Vernon
N.Y.

February 1, 1944
24

My Dearest Darling –
Just finished writing you a V-mail* as I think that is the fastest means of correspondence. However, I don't like the damn stuff as I feel too exposed. There's a possibility of sending mail within the next few days, and I really hope I "can do". I know you must be wondering what has happened to me, but I really am okay. Just haven't run across a mail man lately.

Darling, there is so much I'd like to tell you about, but I'm afraid it all must wait 'til that happy day when we can say – not write – I love you. They tell me there is a war going on, but I sometimes wonder if perhaps what we call war is merely a tragic comedy. You probably can't make much sense out of this rambling, but I'm going a bit unbalanced because I miss you so much and it has only been two months but seems more like two years.

It is getting fairly hard to write as I haven't heard from you in three weeks, and haven't done a thing I can write about. I think of you every minute of the day and wish I were with you. There are plenty of others in the same fix, but they can't feel as strongly as I do. If they did, they would crack under the strain. Guess that places me in the "superman" category. I can hear that reply right now – freshie!

Darling, I've got to run now – eat and relieve the watch – the old routine. I love you with every breath I take and I'll never stop missing you for one second until I am with you again. I adore you, and I'm going to squeeze you mighty tight at the next opportunity. My love to all.

Forever Yours,

Donnie

---

*V-Mail was a standardized mail service created by the U.S. government to help speed up delivery of the volumes of letters that were being sent back and forth. Reduced to microfilm to save space, the content of the letters were blown up again before reaching their destination. Some servicemen, including Donald, distrusted it.[8]

Donald composed the following letter on the eve of Mardy's 21st birthday, while U.S. troops were fighting the Japanese to capture Kwajalein Island.[9] At that time, the *Gatling* was anchored in a lagoon off Majuro Atoll, Marshall Islands.[10] Donald still could not tell Mardy his location, but there was a bit of good news: he was able to send out his letters.

Surely Mardy was relieved when she received Donald's letters confirming he was okay. She may have had friends or acquaintances who lost their husbands, or at the very least she had read about losses in the papers. There she was at home, a pregnant and lonely Navy wife, with no idea of where he was or what he was doing. All this, and she was only about to reach legal voting age. We can only imagine the emotions tumbling around in her head.

And even though Donald alluded to it in this message, Mardy could never have tired of his many declarations of love and longing for her. In fact, they had to be one of the things that kept her going day-to-day.

[No address information available]

3 Feb., 1944

25

My Darling –

The mail finally went out today and I feel loads better knowing that at least a few letters are on the way to "snooks". Right now I'm sitting in the wardroom with all the boys. Stan and Doc are playing chess, Innis is wise-cracking and the radio is blaring – I mean the phonograph. There are many songs that remind me so much of you.

I may use another check $25 for mess bill – so if your books don't balance to the tune of 25 bucks you'll know where it escaped to. If I can stall off the "Doc" – the real one – 'till pay day the check won't be necessary.

Can't tell you where I am, beautiful, but it's a long ways from where I want to be right now. Wonder how long it will be before I don't have to think and say that. The time can't be too short for me, darling.

There are times when I feel like a dolt* writing all my letters in the same vein – how much I want the world at peace and you and I living our own normal lives. However, I know you understand that you and all you do are foremost in my mind every minute of the day.

Right this minute – more than anything in the world I can imagine – I'd like to be splitting our bottle of champagne with Mardets in front of a log fire with all the lights turned off. After that!!!

Darling, I must relieve Bull C. and stay on the ball for the next four hours. Give my love to all. I love you.

Lovingly Yours Forever,

Don

Happy Birthday XXXXX

---

*"A stupid person."[11]

Even though he wasn't able to be with Mardy on her birthday, Donald appeared to be in a jovial mood when he wrote this message, and even joked about his wife's lack of cooking skills. Mardy's January 15 letter telling him the news of her pregnancy still had not reached him.

[No address information available]

Saturday
5 Feb., 1944
26

My Darling –

First of all please accept my sincerest congratulations for your 21ˢᵗ birthday. In other words, I love you and certainly wished every minute of the day yesterday that I could be with you. Hope you had a gay old time and had a drink or three for me.

Angel, your mate right now is suffering from an overdose of sunshine. I sat out in old sol yesterday morning for four hours, and the results were that I feel and look like a par-boiled lobster.

The last letter I received from you was mailed over a month ago, so you see I'm far behind the times as far as your activities are concerned. Gosh, darling, it's a strange world when all I care for is kept so far away and such a deep dark secret.

I just went up to eat dinner, but the squeeze was applied, and I found myself without a seat. However, I'd just as soon write you as eat – except when I'm awful hungry. By the way, darling, on the subject of eating; have you progressed above fried egg sandwiches yet? I don't mean to be sarcastic, 'cause I don't give a darn whether I eat or not when I'm with you. I could live on love for quite some time now. I'm well fortified with food but there is a definite emptiness as far as certain other items are concerned.

Last night I learned how to play cribbage. Ever played? It's a good game for two or four. Won't it be the nuts to have our own house and have friends in for bridge, poker etc. I'd better cease all thoughts in that vein immediately or I'll jump over the side and start swimming, and it's a long way to dog paddle!

According to all reports, the war news seems to be on the bright side. Hope it gets to be a blinding bright very soon. They should fight wars as of old, and have the leaders of each tribe battle it out with bare fists. Not that I'm not patriotic, but the whole mess seems like such damn nonsense now and then.

Darling, once again the time has come to say adieu. My heart and my love come with this letter to the one I adore.

Lovingly Yours Forever,

Don

The following is the last of Donald's letters written during the winter of 1944 to survive. It had been a little more than three months since he and Mardy wed, and Donald had taken to counting each month of their marriage as an anniversary.

[No address information available]

Monday
February 7, 1944
27

Mardy Darling –

Have time for but a very short note. Just time enough to say I love you, adore you, and miss you very, very much.

That sunburn I spoke about in my last letter really turned out to be a corker – so bad, in fact, that I couldn't raise my arms above my head.

Darling, remember if there are long lapses between my letters don't you worry. I know you'll worry some, but not too much. Your old man can take care of himself, and he looks out for No. 1. You are really #1, but when you are not around I take your temporary spot – okay?

Darling we've had three wedding anniversaries already, and stinker that I am you haven't even received a bouquet. I never forget our anniversary, angel, and the 20th of every month for the rest of my life will always be a special day to me. I love you so very much, dearest – far more than I can ever tell you on paper. My love to Gram, Dad and Judy. Keep your chin up and have your Dad give you a big smacker for me.

I'll Love You Forever,

Donnie

CHAPTER SEVEN

The four letters in this chapter were the last of Mardy's messages to survive the war and its aftermath. Given that Donald moved around so much during his service, it is not surprising.

Still living under her parents' roof, Mardy teetered between her roles as their young daughter and a married woman in her first trimester of pregnancy. Concerned about her husband's well-being and hoping for the best, Mardy tried to allay her fears with work, friends, and family.

Mrs. D.E. Storey
Mt. Vernon, N.Y.

Ensign D.E. Storey, U.S.N.
U.S.S. Gatling (D.D. 671)
c/o Fleet Post Office
San Francisco, Calif.

Saturday
2/19/44

My Dearest Darling –
I got two letters from you yesterday, and needless to say I was delighted to hear from you. I got letters 25 and 27, so maybe I'll have another one

coming. I haven't gotten the one about your sunburn yet. I hope it wasn't too bad.

Darling, of course the news is good in some ways, but please, please don't let anything happen to you. Jeepers, if anything ever happened to you – well it's just not going to, that's all.

I didn't do much last night except go to bed because I had to go to work today. Everything was fine until about 12:00. Bobbie* and I went down for our second breakfast about 10:30 and stayed 'till 11:15. Then at 12:00 Mr. S. came in and started giving me all sorts of stuff. He had to take the 1:50 to Houston Tex. or I'd still be there.

I went shopping with Bobbie but I didn't get anything. Just window shopped. That reminds me, darling, please cash a check anytime you feel like it – heavens we have enough money for anything you need. Please darling – take whatever you want.

Dotty and Warren** and Aunt Eddie came for dinner tonight and right now they're all playing games downstairs, but I wanted to write to my O.A.O.*** so here I am up here by myself.

Gosh, but I miss you. It just can't be much longer – you've just got to come home soon.

Well, darling, I'll see you in my dreams –

Yours always,

Mardy

---

*A co-worker and friend.

**Warren was presumably a friend of Mardy's Aunt Dotty.

***One and only.

By March, word had finally gotten to Donald about Mardy's pregnancy. It seems as if he had taken to writing friends with the good news! Meanwhile, Mardy was upset about the income tax she had to pay. She drowned her sorrows in self-care and mused about not being able to write a better letter to the father of her unborn child.

Mrs. D.E. Storey
Mt. Vernon, N.Y.

Ensign D.E. Storey, U.S.N.
U.S.S. Gatling (D.D. 671)
c/o Fleet Post Office
San Francisco, Cal.

Friday
March 10, 1944

Hi darling –
How's my most wonderful, super dooper husband? I hope you've gotten some more rest and will stay wherever you are for a while. It's so nice to hear from you this way.

Phyl just called, and she has heard the news – she was as bad as Judy – she couldn't get over it. Your news really traveled fast darling.

You should see me now, darling. I'm befoodled and befuddled and mad as the dickens. I have to pay $11.87* Income Tax, and I can't figure it out to be any other way but that way. Dad and I have been figuring it out all day and night, but we can't get it to work out any other way. So I'm going to fill out the paper and send the stupid thing off. I'm really lucky – so many kids have a lot to pay, but I only worked about 6 months in '43.

Diddy called me today – Dad and she got in this afternoon and are coming to our house tomorrow to spend the weekend, and then Sunday afternoon Mom, Dad and I are going to a cocktail party with them in New York.

I have to wash my hair tonight, wash two blouses, do my nails, and get some sleep. Tomorrow I go to the dentist again but thank goodness it will be the last time and I only have to have them cleaned.

Darling, I wish I were a poet or that I would write a beautiful letter and tell you just how much I love you, adore you and miss you, but you'll just have to read between the lines, add what I say to it and then multiply it by a million trillion and you'll have a rough idea.

Yours forever and ever –

Mardy

---

*According to online inflation calculators, $11.87 in 1944 is worth about $190 in 2022.

From this message we learn that Mardy had a bad habit of driving around town without a license! This was a behavior Donald heartily disapproved of, as evidenced in some of his later letters to her.

Mrs. D.E. Storey
Mt. Vernon, N.Y.

Ensign D.E. Storey, U.S.N.
U.S.S. Gatling (D.D. 671)
c/o Fleet Post Office
San Francisco, Calif.

[Postmarked March 17, 1944]
Saturday
[Letter not dated]

Hi darling –

I just sneaked off for a minute or two to drop my O.A.O. a line. How's life aboard the RBG at this point? I wish you could be here with us, darling, but we'll have so many parties when you get home.

I finished up at the dentist's this morning, and now my teeth are all pretty again – I washed my hair too and now I'm all dressed up. I drove down (without my license) and got Diddy and Dad and then we spent the rest of the afternoon talking about you and catching up all our news for the past two weeks. (to be continued)

Hi – I'm now writing in bed, so please excuse if I wobble off sometimes. We had a lot of fun tonight, we went up to Dominick's for dinner and I had Filet Mignon. We didn't see anyone we knew, but we had an awful lot of fun just being together.

Here I am back in the same day, and I'm sleepy again. I'm in Judy's room because Dad and Diddy use mine. Honestly, it's so much fun having them here. I just love them so much, but not half as much as I love you. In fact no one loves anyone as much as I love you.

Well snooks, I'm awfully sleepy, and I want to get to sleep before Judy comes home so she won't put the light on and keep me up all night.

Always and always – Yours,
Mardy

In mid March, Mardy was still in the process of telling people the exciting news of her pregnancy, and appears to have celebrated over the weekend by having numerous cocktails. At that time in our history, alcohol was considered safe to drink during pregnancy. She may have been feeling some lingering effects when she put these words on paper, as she made several errors!

Mrs. D.E. Storey
Mt. Vernon, N.Y.

Ensign D.E. Storey, U.S.N.
U.S.S. Gatling (D.D. 671)
c/o Fleet Post Office
San Francisco, Calif.

Sunday
March 19, 1944

My Dearest Darling –
I miss you and love you absolute millions – you know it's been so long since I saw you – the longest time since we've been going together – much, much too long. I don't mind too awful much when I realize that you're not in the air corps, or a marine,* and that someday soon you'll be coming home for good and we will have so much ~~firn~~ fun. (excuse)

Phyl came up for the weekend and we had such a good time. I just think she's the darlingest girl. I met her Saturday after work and we met Dody** and went to the Commodore for cocktails and lunch. We all met in Grand Central and I met Dody first and broke the news to her and honestly I've never seen anyone that was so affected – she couldn't say anything – all she could do was hang on to me and I thought she'd never stop crying. She's so excited I'm going to have an awful time keeping her down to ~~the~~ (excuse) earth and she got me so excited – we had some time.

We had "side-cars" – have you ever had one? Golly they're marvelous – we only had one and it's a darn good thing – they're plenty potent. Then Phyl and I came ~~one~~ (excuse) home. (I'm making a million errors – please excuse all from now on.) We had more cocktails and dinner and mother had to work at Fort Slocum with the Red Cross so Daddy, Judy, Phyl and I went to the movies to see "A Guy Named Joe" with Spencer Tracy and Irene Dunne – it was simply marvelous. I hope you get to see it out there.

Today we got up nice and late and we went to church and then Eddie came over and we had cocktails and then dinner and we went for a ride and then we came home and now Phyl and I are in bed writing to our O.A.O's. Well, darling, I'm being very un-hostess like – Phyl finished her letter quite a while ago so I'd better close.

I love you my darling so very much – and can't wait until the day you will come home.

Goodnight, darling –

Love always,

Mardy

---

*Mardy may have thought these branches of service were more dangerous than the Navy. Percentage wise, there were more Marine casualties than Navy causalities during World War II. And there were great losses suffered within the Air Corps, whose casualty statistics were combined with the Army's.[1]

**Dody was Mardy's mother's cousin.

CHAPTER EIGHT

Big Changes

From mid-February until the end of April 1944, none of Donald's letters survived. During that time, he regularly tasted the terror and uncertainty of war. In mid-February, U.S. carriers launched air strikes on Micronesia's Truk Lagoon, a major Japanese bastion housing their ships and planes.[1] In the days that followed, the *Gatling*'s formation endured enemy air attacks and shot down enemy planes. On February 22, the destroyer survived several close calls, including near misses by bombs and a crashed plane. One Japanese plane shot down by the *Gatling* crashed on her starboard quarter.[2] This was almost eight months to the day before kamikaze pilots started intentionally crashing into American warships.

By mid March, the formation had travelled all the way to New Hebrides in the South Pacific, and on March 29, they survived another attack by the Japanese. They ended the month north of the Equator again, when U.S. carriers launched air strikes on Palau and the island of Yap.

April saw a return to Majuro. By the end of the month, the *Gatling* was still in the vicinity of the Marshall Islands. On April 29 and 30, air strikes were launched again on Truk Lagoon.[3]

As usual, Donald didn't hint about any of the fighting in his messages. Instead, he wrote about movies, the upcoming presidential election, and his need for some snapshots. We also discover what sex he thought their baby would be!

The following was written as one letter, but on two separate dates.

[No address information available]

Friday
April 28th, 1944
at Sea
67

My darling –

Hope to get these letters off soon, as I know you are probably beginning to wonder where your errant husband is and what he is doing. Well, sweets, he doesn't know where he is, and he is not doing much. Just bounding around from wave to wave.

We had an awful picture last night called "The Fighting SeaBees".* It is one of those Saturday thrillers which make up part of the 5 or 6 hour Saturday afternoon matinee. Strongly advise you to give this one the go by.

Darling, how about doing me a big favor? If you haven't any snapshots of yourself – as you have so often reminded me – please steal a roll of film someplace and snap a few, have them developed, and enclose same in a letter. Do this and I promise to love, honor, and (ahem – OK. I'll obey!) you now and forever. I promised that over six months ago, but I'll reaffirm my vows – I do it every day anyhow. S'nuff, s'nuff – anyhow, I would appreciate some snapshots, beautiful.

Darling, I must "chow down" so I'll bid you a fond adieu for this evening. I love you, dearest,

Don

Saturday
April 29, 1944
at Sea

My darling –

Hi precious! Thought I would continue on the same paper as yesterday's lines were few. Afraid the same will apply today as I've about run out of writing subjects – only for the present – and my bean ain't working too sharp.

We received some mail yesterday – first class and packages, no air mail – and all I got were two church papers. Hope to meet the flying mailman soon and collect some more letters from my O.A.O.

We had another movie last night – for a change! This time it was "Good Morning Judge",** and surprisingly enough it wasn't a bad show. Guess we are one of a very few tin cans that show movies at sea. You go crazy without some sort of relaxation, and "Old Lady" R. doesn't believe in gambling. That is undoubtedly a good thing for our bank roll, no doubt.

How's the presidential situation coming?*** Suppose you will vote – you can cast one for me too! I don't know much about it, but I don't want Thomas E. Dewey in the White House.

How is "snooks"? Hope the little one isn't troubling you. Give <u>him</u> my best love – aside from you I love "snooks" best. Guess that wraps things up for tonight, darling. Sweet dreams and a long kiss to the one I love.

Forever yours,

Don

---

*A 1944 film starring John Wayne and Susan Hayward.[4]

**A 1943 comedy starring Dennis O'Keefe, Louise Allbritton, and Mary Beth Hughes.[5]

***In 1944, President Franklin D. Roosevelt was running for an unprecedented fourth term against Thomas E. Dewey, the Governor of New York. Roosevelt would go on to win by a landslide.[6]

Sometime in early June, Donald completed his service aboard the USS *Gatling*. On June 15, 1944, soon after the Allied invasion of Normandy across the world in France, Donald departed San Francisco en route to the Naval Submarine Base New London in Groton, Connecticut, to attend sub school in preparation for his next assignment. It is possible he asked for this transfer to be close to Mardy, who was in her third trimester of pregnancy.

Donald arrived at New London on July 1. For ten precious months between July 1944 and March 1945, Mardy and Donald made a temporary home there in rented quarters.

As the birth of their baby drew near, Mardy travelled back to Mt. Vernon, and on August 28, 1944, little Margery (Marcy) Storey was born at Mount Vernon Hospital. Donald was present at the birth, but had to report back to the submarine base the next day. He sent the following letter after he arrived home, as he awaited the return of Mardy with their firstborn.

DE Storey, Ensign, USN
New London, Conn.

Mrs. D.E. Storey
Mt. Vernon Hospital
Mt. Vernon
N.Y.

Tuesday night
August 29, 1944

My Precious –
I'm sitting here, drink in hand and imagine you're right next to me. Won't be long now, however. Darling, I certainly do love you and "little snook", and if it were not that I'd collapse, I'd be on my way to you both right now. Must admit I'm sort of tired tonight. My handwriting probably shows that.

The trip back last night wasn't bad, and I managed to collar a little sleep between changing trains. Got home at 4:30 on the dot. Hope you had a comfortable night – "Little snook" too!

My ring finally arrived, and it looks fine. Believe it's better looking than when it had the garnet in it. No laundry as yet this week!

I just bumped into Mary and she was all questions. Sends you her best and says she is looking forward to your coming back – me too!!

How did our daughter look today? I think she's a real cutie – sure takes after her mother.

Dearest, guess that's all the news. All my love and thoughts are with you both, and I'm counting the seconds 'til Saturday. Be sure and take it easy so I can spend the whole day with you Sunday.

Devotedly Yours Forever,

Donnie

P.S. XXXX

X – For "little snook"

PART TWO

CHAPTER NINE

The Submarine

According to documentation found with the letters, Donald ended his studies at submarine school in late August 1944, and in September went to work on the fitting out of a newly constructed submarine at the Electric Boat Company in Groton, Connecticut—the USS *Carbonero* SS-337. On March 21, 1945, the sub departed New London with Donald aboard, and served with the Fleet Sonar School at Key West, Florida until mid-April.[1] By that time, Donald had been promoted to a lieutenant junior grade.

While stationed in Key West, he and Mardy spent two weeks together, while her parents took care of the baby. When Donald wrote the following letter, they had just ended their visit. Parting seemed to be getting harder for the couple.

DE Storey, Lieut (jg) USN
USS Carbonero (SS 337)
c/o Fleet Post Office
New York, N.Y.

Mrs. D.E. Storey
Mount Vernon
New York

Thursday Night
12 April, 1945

My Dearest Darling –

I still cannot realize that my whole life rode away a few hours ago. I'm sure you will be waiting for me at the next port of call. There just is no other way – not a fair one at least.

Darling, I hope the ride atop a suitcase wasn't too bad. Know it was unpleasant in more respects than one! And world what have you done to us now!

Writing to you is certainly not going to be any strain. Millions of things to ask you, tell you and discuss with you are running through my head at this very instant. Above all, I want to tell you how very very proud I was of the stiff upper lip you kept throughout the trial and tribulations. If you hadn't, I'm sure I would have done a little weeping myself. Darling, I love you with every "corpuscle" in my body.

George and I stumbled slowly back after my life left, and not one word issued from the lips of either one of us. I couldn't talk as the lungs in my throat made it feel as though it were about to give at the seams. All went as it was planned and as it has only been a few hours since we said "so long for a while", all I've done is stare into space and force a very untasty few mouthfuls down my gullet.

Darling, one of the boys just stuck his head in the wardroom and said President Roosevelt is dead. If so, it will certainly be a terrific loss to the United States and the whole world. Looks like your Dad was right when he said Truman would finish out the fourth term.* That is not to my liking at all. Guess it's true as they just turned on the radio. April 12, 1945 is a bad day all around.

Dearest, I am so glad we had those two weeks in Key West. I thoroughly enjoyed every minute – but then I can't ever remember a minute of my life with you that I haven't enjoyed to the fullest. If two people were ever created for one another, I know well enough who they were – Margery and Donald.

Wonder what you are doing right now? Wish you were running to the kitchen to try and save the burnt potatoes. Don't know why I must sit here and torture us both with memories like that, but it serves to ease the intense pain in my heart to put down on paper that which I treasure so deeply.

Bet my boots T'Nook will be glad to see her mommie. I sort of suspect that mommie will be glad to see her too! Give the little "stinker" a big old hug and a kiss for me the moment you finish reading this. Tell her to return both with plenty of gusto – just as if she were I.

"Love of my life", until tomorrow at this time I'll bid you a fond adieu. I love you dearest, above all else and miss you terrifically already.

Forever and Ever Yours,

Donnie

---

*President Franklin Delano Roosevelt (FDR), whose health had been declining for years, died less than three months into his fourth term, having guided the country through both the Great Depression and World War II. Harry S. Truman, his vice president, succeeded him.[2]

Besides being dangerous, life on a submarine could be lonely and claustrophobic. There were few creature comforts aboard. Electricity and fresh water (made from sea water) had to be used conservatively. There were limited showers and toilets. As a result, the atmosphere was often hot, dark, stuffy, and smelly.[3] Donald, however, seemed to enjoy his first days on the sub over his time on a destroyer. In this letter, he spoke fondly of his time in the sun and the good chow. But nothing, not even steak and cherry pie, could distract him from longing for his family.

DE Storey, Lieut (jg) USN
USS Carbonero (SS 337)
c/o Fleet Post Office
New York, N.Y.

Mrs. D.E. Storey
Mount Vernon
New York

Friday Evening
April 13th, 1945

Dearest Angel Cake –
Right now you are just 180° out of phase – going north while I go south. Turn around in a hurry! I still cannot comprehend the truth which is staring me in the face – the fact that I won't see you – not for a matter of days but of months. Darling, I guess I'm just made for one thing – to live with you. I sure don't like this living alone.

I didn't rise until after 9 o'clock this morning as I had the 10–2 last night. The rest of the day was spent in drills and an afternoon watch. Nothing exciting except I almost lost the bubble on a dive this afternoon – Friday the 13th I guess.

Again tonight I am listening to the news about the President. It certainly must have been a shock to the country. Wonder what Truman will turn out to be in the way of a President.

Tomorrow morning you will see little T'nook. Wish I were going to be there – I will be there with my thoughts and my heart. Wouldn't miss the reunion of the two I love best for anything.

After an afternoon of sunshine, my arms are looking quite brown. Afraid they couldn't compare with yours though. You really looked healthy and beautiful after your two weeks of Florida sunshine. Darling, you should have stayed for dinner tonight! Everything you like from fillet mignon with mushrooms to cherry pie.

I haven't invested one single nickel in our "one armed bandit".* Aren't you proud of my thrift? I wouldn't lay any bets on just how long the temptation will be resisted, however. You know, "love bug", it has been so long since I've written a letter that I find it hard to spell words right or punctuate. You and I don't need to spell or punctuate do we? Pardon just one minute!!

Back again to say I love you. My new pen tells me it would rather write that phrase than any it has written thus far in its career. By the way, the pen is writing very well. Everything works well that has anything to do with "my ole woman".

I still have on the pants I had when you left – and the rip is becoming larger all the time. Good opportunity to try out my spankin new sewing outfit.

Until tomorrow night about this time I'll say bye bye with all my love to "Angel pudding" and T'nook". Our love is such a perfect one, and our life will be too when all is calm and peaceful.

Forever and Ever Yours,

Donnie

XXXXXXXOOOOOO   XXXXXXXOOOO

For Mardy   For T'nook

---

*A slot machine.

Aboard the *Carbonero*, Donald was a torpedo and gunnery officer and an engineering officer. In this next letter, he wrote about some of the crew's war exercises. At the time, the submarine was still in port in Florida, and Mardy had arrived back home with her parents and reunited with the baby.

DE Storey, Lieut (jg) USN
USS Carbonero (SS 337)
c/o Fleet Post Office
New York, N.Y.

Mrs. D.E. Storey
Mount Vernon
New York

Saturday Night
April 14th, 1945

My Beloved Darling,
You are undoubtedly very tired tonight after the trip, and probably just a weeny bit nervous being with your parents again for the first time. Since we said so long for a while, I have followed you in my mind every minute. Once in a great while I really feel sorry for us as we love one another just too darn much.

I had the 6–10 watch this morning, and came off watch only to be caught in a swirl of drills which lasted until late this afternoon. After I cleaned up a bit – changed my skivvies – I had chow and read a story in Cosmo. Not a very exciting day but we can mark it down as one more day towards the day we are both waiting for. Last night I lay awake for almost an hour talking to you. We talked about T'Nook, the "Beast",* where our money goes, and how lucky we are.

Everything has run smoothly in the Torpedo and Gunnery department for the last few days – for which I am duly thankful – and if same holds I suppose I must become energetic and get "hot" on my notebook.** The "Skip" is worried tonight as he is supposed to hold church services tomorrow in memory of the President. Says he has never held them before and doesn't know quite where to begin. Hope you will have a softer resting place for your knees tomorrow than we had the past two Sundays. That was a lot of fun – those two Sunday mornings at church together. I also remember how you "took charge and marched off" from me last Sunday – stinker!!

How does little T'Nook look? Did she recognize you? How many teeth has she got? Have her high chair, bassinette etc. arrived as yet? I have a million of the same, but I know they will be answered as soon as I get mail.

I am going to lay down for an hour so I'll be on my toes during my four hour trick on the bridge. Until tomorrow, darling all my love, devotion, and thoughts are with you and T'Nook.

Ever and Forever Yours,

Donnie

---

*The couple's nickname for their car.

**Donald referred to his notebook in several letters. A notebook detailing all operating systems of the sub was one of the tasks he had to complete to earn his qualification in submarines—a requirement for all serving aboard.[4] According to the U.S. Navy, this qualification "represents an intensive personal effort to meet the high standards and special requirements of submarine duty." [5]

DE Storey, Lieut (jg) USN
USS Carbonero (SS 337)
c/o Fleet Post Office
New York, N.Y.

Mrs. D.E. Storey
Mount Vernon
New York

Sunday Evening
April 15, 1945

My Dearest Darling –
The past three days have been long and lonesome. I wasn't ready to leave you, and I'm sure ready to turn around and head for you and T'nook now! It is almost like living in a dream – a bad dream – and I wish I would wake up and find you sleeping alongside me.

All in all I feel very healthy in body but not in heart. My heart is sick, and I don't believe it will be completely well again until Snookie, T'Nook and Huggy are keeping house together – along with the "Beast", "Lucy", and "Cutie Pie" of course.* We have nicknames for more things. This proves we live in a world all of our own. I honestly believe, darling, that the three of us would be completely content and happy together if we never had contact with another human being. In a few years, one member would undoubtedly not be so content – I believe you and I would though.

I am rather incoherent tonight. Hope to mail this tomorrow, and guess I'd better write one to Mother and Dad. My love to Gram, Judy, and Ernie.** Every bit of me travels with this letter to you and T'Nook. All my love, devotion, thoughts, and wants –
Forever and Ever Yours,
Donnie

---

*Huggy was probably Mardy's pet name for Donald. Cutie Pie may have been another nickname for the baby. It is not known who or what Lucy was.

**Mardy's father.

Submarine itineraries were highly classified during the war—even today it is difficult to pinpoint the *Carbonero*'s precise location by date. However, by the time Donald penned this next letter, his sub was probably conducting torpedo exercises at Balboa, Canal Zone, in Panama City, Panama, about 875 miles south of Cuba.[6]

DE Storey, Lieut (jg) USN
USS Carbonero (SS 337)
c/o Fleet Post Office
New York, N.Y.

Mrs. D.E. Storey
Mount Vernon
N.Y.

Monday Night
April 16th, 1945
In Port

My Dearest Darling –
Good evening, angel. Hope it's not as uncomfortably warm in Mt. Vernon this evening as it is here. I have the duty, and also have to load "fish". Hope I'll be able to get ashore and purchase a few trinkets sometime before we leave.

Mail came in today, but I garnered but one letter from mother. I didn't expect any at all this soon so don't feel bad. Larry and I are the only ones aboard tonight, and he has turned in. Exciting night don't you think?

Darling, time does not pass that I'm not wishing with all my heart we were together. I especially miss you when the sun goes down. I know darn well when that happens I should be with my wife and daughter.

I got up this morning at 4:45 and it doesn't appear like I'll get to bed much before that tomorrow morning. I'd rather work long and hard as it keeps my mind occupied somewhat. No matter what I do though I can never lose you in my thoughts for one instant. I don't ever want to.

How is little T'Nook? Does she miss her old man? I sure would like to pinch her fat little rump, and maybe have a good belly laugh with her while you attempted to listen to the radio. Remember that one particular night when she was standing on my tummy and giggling away?

Until tomorrow, darling, I'll meet you in my dreams and my love and thoughts are with you both as always. I love you, my darling.

Forever and Ever Yours,

Donnie

On April 17, Donald was thinking about his hunt for the perfect doll for little Margery. He was less forthcoming in telling Mardy about some presents he bought for her. Back home, Mardy was saving up to complete the baby's room, and preparing to take her for an extended visit to Donald's parents.

The next day, Donald continued his message on the same air mail paper. As he yearned to be close with his wife, he reminisced about an innocent yet intimate activity they used to enjoy together.

DE Storey, Lieut (jg) USN
USS Carbonero (SS 337)
c/o Fleet Post Office
New York, N.Y.

Mrs. D.E. Storey
Mount Vernon
New York

Tuesday Evening
April 17th, 1945
In Port

My Dearest Darling –
Hello "angel de pangel". I bought you a few trinkets this morning at ships service, but will wait to mail them until I acquire a doll for T'Nook. I think you will really like what I bought, and I won't tell you what it is, so there too!

How is everything coming along, honey? It won't be too long now before you will have enough money in the bank to buy snooks a crib and playpen. Mother said in her letter that she is getting a crib so you two will visit for a long time.

Darling, I've got lots to do, so will sign off and continue tomorrow as I can't mail this 'till then anyhow. I love you dearest, and want you by my side – if not closer – from now 'til eternity. Say goodnight to T'Nook and give her a squeeze for me.

Forever and Ever, Your
Donnie

Wednesday Afternoon
April 18th, 1945

My Darling Wife –

Another day gone by until we will be together again. So far today, I've been quite busy – frantic you might say – as the torpedo and gunnery has been doing its stuff. So far so good, however.

We saw three tremendous sharks yesterday afternoon, shot at them, but I'm afraid didn't cause them too much discomfort.

I am very anxious to receive some letters from you and hear about your trip home, T'Nook, etc. I'd much rather receive you in the mail, then you could tell me about everything personally. Perhaps we could have a party!* What a terrible thing for me to say! Hey, angel, my hair needs washing – bet yours does too. What say we declare tomorrow night "hair washing night". Remember how we used to pour the cold water on one another? You could dump a gallon of ice water on me right now and I would love it. Not just because of the heat – but because you would be there to laugh at me.

Darling, they are calling for me again so I must say adieu. I love you with all my heart and soul – I'm existing but I wouldn't call it living in the true sense of the word. My love to all but especially to you. Until tomorrow, then.

I love you,
Donnie
P.S. XXXXXXXXXXXX

---

*Donald's code word for making love.

DE Storey, Lieut (jg) USN
USS Carbonero (SS 337)
c/o Fleet Post Office
New York, N.Y.

Mrs. D.E. Storey
Mount Vernon
New York

Friday Evening
April 20th, 1945
#1

My Dearest Darling,

As of tonight, I am starting to number my letters so you can keep track of any missed and stuff. I didn't write last night – for which I beg your humble pardon – because we didn't finish up until after midnight – training I mean – and I was dog tired.

As yet, I haven't received any mail from you. Expect to receive some in a day or so when we return to port. A mail boat came out today, but all I received was a package of Gillette razor blades, 50 in all.

I'm still waiting to get ashore to buy a doll for T'Nook so I can mail you both a package. I would like to wrap myself up, put on a big stamp, and come home First Class Air Mail.

The training we are getting here is excellent, and it is all for the T & G department which so far has performed excellently in my opinion, but then I am probably prejudiced!

Sure glad it is finally getting around to the end of the month so you will have money to support you and T'Nook. Wish I could help you pick out a crib. Be sure and buy a soft mattress for our babe. She is so darn cute she at least deserves a nice soft mattress.

Darling, it doesn't seem possible that it has been only 8 days since you left. It certainly feels more like 8 months to me. When 8 months has really passed, I intend to be with you or at least coming your way in the near future. They can't keep me away from you any longer than that. The war news looks so good that I sort of feel it will all be over in a year at the most.

Until tomorrow, dearest, I'll go on loving you with all my heart and soul. Give T'Nook my love and tell her to be a good girl.

Forever and Ever Yours,

Donnie

XXXX

At the time the following letter was written, Donald was still in Panama wrapping up training. It wouldn't be long before the *Carbonero* would depart for Pearl Harbor.[7]

Donald hadn't received any letters from Mardy since they parted, and he was starting to worry, which may have led him to reminisce about their time together in New London. He settled on a doll for the baby, and as Mother's Day approached, he was preparing to mail several presents to his family before his location changed. Not surprisingly, he continued his campaign to get Mardy to stop driving without a license.

DE Storey, Lieut (jg) USN
USS Carbonero (SS 337)
c/o F.P.O., N.Y., N.Y.

Mrs. D.E. Storey
Mount Vernon
New York

Monday Night
April 23, 1945
In Port
#3

My Dearest Beloved –
Good evening, lovely lady, and how are you? I have missed you very much of late, especially since I won't receive any mail from you until we reach our next port of call. It seems as if the post office department has it in for me. The least they could do is send me one of your letters so I would at least know you arrived beside T'Nook safe and sound. I almost said arrived home, but you and I know that your folks' home is not your home any more. It is merely a temporary residence until we hang our pajamas on the same hook again.

I finally got your package off today, but there is one gift missing which I will enclose in my next letter – tomorrow to be exact. I don't think much of the doll for T'Nook, but it is at least original and typical of the place from whence it comes. I enclosed a present for mother in the package which I hope she will like. There was so much I wanted to buy for you, darling, but the money factor wasn't anything to brag about. However, I think you will like what I did manage to send. The present in the cigar box is from T'Nook and I for Mother's Day. How does it seem to be receiving Mother's Day presents? Personally, I am heartily in favor of you being a mother, but above all I'm in love with my wife. Darling, I can write I love you a thousand times, but it definitely is not the same as being able to whisper "I love you" in your ear.

Right now Larry and I are sitting in the ward room writing letters. Bud is asleep on the couch, and George is wrapping a package to Mae. The rest are ashore. I'm going ashore tomorrow afternoon to find a charm for your bracelet, but I'm not going to stay over tomorrow night. I would rather stay aboard where it is peaceful and quiet and write a letter to my dream girl. Darling, I need you so very much. You are my life, and without you by my side nothing has rhyme nor reason. Our months in New London together were so wonderful that now it often seems as if we were living in a dream castle. Then I suddenly remember the Christmas tree lamp by my chair and I can clearly see the old house on Williams Street.

I suppose that cute little rascal of ours is trying to walk harder and harder each and every day. Soon now you will be able to put a swimsuit on her and watch her get tanned. Can you imagine little T'Nook with a suntan?

So far I haven't had much chance to work on my notebook, but hope to have it practically done during the same lapse of time in which Bob L. did his. By the way, darling, you can change my P. O. address when you receive this.

Our training period was highly successful, and I was quite proud of the way my boys performed. As a matter of fact, I did a fairly good job myself. Just lucky I guess.

Darling, have you taken any steps towards a driver's license? Don't forget that "The Beast" is for your use, but only after you have a license! You probably won't have too much in the way of gas now that we can't apply for "B" tickets.* The Beast certainly was a wonderful investment. We had plenty of use and pleasure out of that old heaping tuna. Remember our N.Y. and Boston trips?

Until tomorrow evening, angel, every bit of my love comes to you on every wave. My thoughts are always with you and T'Nook – now and forevermore. I love you both dearly and need you with me wherever I go. Goodnight, dearest.

I love you, I love you.

Donnie

XXXXXX

---

*During World War II, gas was rationed for fuel conservation as well as for tire conservation because of the rubber shortage. The B gas ration ticket, or sticker, was worth up to eight gallons a week, but the government primarily issued it to business owners. The A sticker, which was far more common, was for the general public and allowed motorists four gallons a week. The rationing continued until August, 1945.[8]

Donald wrote this message the night before the *Carbonero*'s departure for Pearl Harbor. He took advantage of his final day to go ashore and bought a charm for Mardy, but, as in many of his letters, his concern about finances surfaced.

As time went on, Donald fell more in love with his little girl, and asked about her often, remembering the short but sweet moments he was able to have with her before he was deployed. As for his wife, if he had any inhibitions before, the romantic playfulness in his writing demonstrated they had evaporated.

DE Storey, Lieut (jg) USN
USS Carbonero (SS 337)
c/o F.P.O., N.Y., N.Y.

Mrs. D.E. Storey
Mount Vernon
New York

Tuesday Evening
April 24th, 1945
In Port
#4

My Dearest Darling –

The end of another day finds me no nearer to the ones I love, but there is at least some small consolation in the fact that I am no farther away tonight than I was last night. Afraid I won't be able to write the same tomorrow night. Consequently, darling, you may not receive any more mail for a few weeks.

Larry and I went ashore this morning to take a look at the shops. I went merely to take a look, as I am financially embarrassed (to say the least) at present. However, after clomping around for what must have been at least fifteen miles and attempting to make 100 shop keepers understand what I wanted, I at last found the enclosed charm. I am sorry it is not just what you want – a moveable one I mean – but the selection was truly limited. Plenty of perfume and alligator bags for sale, but no charms. Anyhow, the whole idea is that this little charm and those to follow at infrequent intervals are small tokens right from my heart. They are attempting to be a symbol of my love for you, but if they were magnified one billion times I do not believe they would be as big in comparison as my love for you is and always will be.

We returned around 1 o'clock this afternoon and then became involved in a softball game which the Carbonero handily won 11–2! Larry is writing a letter in the wardroom, Jess is reading "Forever Amber",* and what I'm doing you have already guessed – trying to make love, long distance, on paper to the most beautiful, most gorgeous, most se— little eyeful I've ever met. I must admit that there are far more satisfactory methods for making love than this one I am forced to adopt – for the time being only! Would it not be wonderful to have a party just about right now?

As I've told you before, I haven't received even one letter, and will not have the pleasure above all pleasures of reading one until we are far removed from here. Bet you can't guess where that will be! Not much you can't!

Darling, tell T'Nook I love her and miss her. Also tell her I am sorry I did not send her more presents, but I just couldn't find a thing for her that was within my financial range. I hope the little rascal misses me a little now and then. I say "good morning little T'Nook" to her picture each and every day. The funny part is in that picture she is smiling just like she used to in the morning. I can almost hear her gurgle.

I just put some records on the vic. I've looked all over the boat for a recording of our song, but no can find. I must pick one up somewhere. I had one on the Rattlin Battlin but it was a "stinker".

I am so darned anxious to hear all about you and T'Nook – what you've been doing etc. She must be becoming better company every day now, and I'll bet she is being spoiled rotten. That's one thing I never did – not much! Remember those few nights we sat around and barked at one another trying to get her to cry herself to sleep. Somebody sure handed us blarney when they advanced that idea.

Well, darling, until tomorrow night around this time I'll be thinking of you constantly and loving you with every breath I take. I do love you so much, sweetheart, and once again am living only for the day we are together again as one in mind, body, and thought. Give T'Nook a big kiss – wish I could give you both a super dooper.

I'll Love You Always,

Donnie

XXXXXX

Forever Amber was written by Kathleen Winsor and published in 1944. At the time, the best seller was considered to be scandalous, and in America it was banned in 14 states. Teenage girls read the novel as an initiation into adulthood.[9]

On April 27, the *Carbonero* was en route to Pearl Harbor.[10] During the previous two days, Donald had been preoccupied with his duties to get underway, but very sweetly intimated to Mardy that she was always with him. It would be two more weeks until he would be able to receive any letters from her, and this reality contributed to his feeling of emptiness.

DE Storey, Lieut (jg) USN
USS Carbonero (SS 337)
c/o F.P.O., San Francisco, Cal.

Mrs. D.E. Storey
Mount Vernon
New York

Friday Night
April 27, 1945
at Sea
#6

My Darling –
First of all, I must apologize for not writing last night, but there just wasn't any time. I will try to see that it doesn't happen again, however. In spite of the fact that I didn't have a chance to write last evening, I talked to you for a few minutes before I went to sleep. I went to sleep with a smile on my face 'cause you just had said you love me.

The last two days have been very full. I am now standing top watches along with Al and Larry. On the whole, everything has been going along smoothly. Sometimes I'm sort of leery because everything has worked out so well for me. Practically everything I do seems to be right. Lady Luck has been smiling on me since the day I married you – that day she was really beaming – radiant you might say.

I still haven't started on my notebook, but in my capacity as professor of the forward torpedo room etc. for the enlisted men, I find I am learning a lot about the boat I didn't know myself!

We had mackerel for supper tonight, and all I could think of was our

Friday night suppers of scrambled eggs on toast and beans. They sure were good.

This afternoon we ran into a school of porpoises. There must have been over 200 in all, and they put on quite a show – jumping, splashing etc. Someday, darling, I hope you and I can watch scenes such as that from the deck rail of some nice luxurious passenger liner. We might even take that cute little T'Nook along.

I can't wait to hear from you, but it will be two weeks yet so I might as well take it easy, Jackson. Seems like such an eternity since we were together. I love you far too much to have the slightest peace of mind when I am away from you. T'Nook, you and I make such an attractive family that it is bad for public morale to separate us. Sounds good, anyhow!

Until tomorrow, sweetheart, I bid you both a very fond goodnight. I love my two girls, and, darling, I need you near me so very very much.

I Love You, Love You, Love You and could Squeeze You Passionately!
Donnie
XXXXXXX
Xxxxxxx
For T'Nookie

DE Storey, Lieut (jg) USN
USS Carbonero (SS 337)
c/o F.P.O., San Francisco, Cal.

Mrs. D.E. Storey
Mount Vernon
New York

Saturday Evening
April 28th, 1945
at Sea
#7

My Dearest Darling –

Another day gone, and the end of it finds me quite tired. Three hours sleep was all I managed to garner last night. Not enough for huggy as you well know. Expect to do much better tonight, however.

Shaved this afternoon for the first time since we left port, but I left on the makings of a small Van Dyke! You would probably toss me out on my ear if you could see me. I hope not, and somehow I think you might let me stick around for a while. How about it!

Wonder what you are doing tonight? That's the hardest part, not knowing what you and T'Nookie are doing.

Last night was a beauty – full moon, calm sea, etc., but I would have traded it and a hundred finer nights for one, cold, rainy night in New London with you and T'Nook.

We saw two large whales this afternoon. One was so close you could look into his eyes. Both of them submerged as they came abeam.

Angel, it is time to go on watch so I must say goodnight. Now and always all my love is for you and T'Nook.

I love you,
Donnie
XXXXX

The baby was nearing a year old, and Donald was counting each month as her birthday. His prayers for a swift end to the war were becoming more regular, especially since there was hope on the horizon, buoyed by the execution of the leader of one of the Axis powers.

DE Storey, Lieut (jg) USN
USS Carbonero (SS 337)
c/o F.P.O., San Francisco, Cal.

Mrs. D.E. Storey
Mount Vernon
New York

Monday Evening
April 30th, 1945
#8

My Darling –
I didn't have a minute to call my own yesterday, and was up all night last night so I didn't get a chance to sit down and tell you how much I adore you. From the looks of things, tonight is going to be another long one. This training is sure rugged!

Darling, I have ants in my pants waiting to at least receive some letters from you. No one on here knows whether his wife arrived home from Key West without difficulty. The postal authorities sure didn't do right by us.

I forgot to tell you to say happy birthday to T'Nookie for me in my last letter – tell her I am sorry the birthday greetings are belated. Just think, the little stinker is eight months old! Those months we three spent together certainly passed quickly, and these next few months will undoubtedly drag by like Father Time.

I hope your package arrives soon, and all in one piece. Wish I could watch you open it. I had quite a time wrapping it up – I'm so skilled at that sort of thing.

What did you think about Mussolini getting bumped off?* That was a surprise. The war news certainly has a rosy tint at present. Let's both pray it continues to move as swiftly and successfully to a close as it has the past two weeks. I want no part of this being away from you business. I don't care for it one particle. You see, my love, I love you, and don't like this life of no kisses, no hugs, no diapers to change, no sleepy snookies to wake up, no afternoon shopping – could go on for hours but what I really mean is no you.

Darling, I hate to say good night, but I have to get up in two hours so perhaps for now I had better sign off. All my love, devotion, and heart is with you always.

I Adore You,

Donnie

XXXXX

---

*Benito Mussolini, creator of Italy's Fascist Party and dictator of the country, was aligned with Germany during the war. With the Allies closing in and his own people uprising against him, Mussolini fled Milan in late April, 1945, but was quickly captured by Italian anti-fascist partisans. He was executed April 28, 1945.[11]

CHAPTER TEN

Germany Surrenders

As May began, the *Carbonero* was continuing on its way toward Pearl Harbor, in the U.S. territory of Hawaii. A day earlier, April 30, Adolf Hitler committed suicide.[1] Germany was on the precipice of surrender, but the end of the war was still months away.

DE Storey, Lieut (jg) USN
USS Carbonero (SS 337)
c/o F.P.O., San Francisco, Cal.

Mrs. D.E. Storey
Mount Vernon
New York

May 1st, 1945
at Sea
Tuesday Evening
#9

My Dearest Darling –
How are you? It must be starting to warm up around home now. I would have to miss the spring, but I'm so darn glad we didn't have to say goodbye in the middle of winter.

I'm glad to see the end of the month roll around in one respect. My two girls will now at least have enough money to buy a soda now and then. Guess when you get through buying a crib and paying bills there won't be too much left. Whatever you do, darling, don't spare either T'Nook or yourself anything you want or need. I believe you'll find we will save money hand over foot. We won't worry about it at any rate.

Dearest, I wish I could tell you "I love you", but I imagine that for now I must be content to write I love you. I do love you, darling, above and beyond everything on the earth.

Everything is running smoothly, but I'm not in a very nice humor this evening, and do not appreciate the sea, the navy, or anything pertaining to same. All in all, darling, I'm homesick, lonely, and lovesick.

Darling, this has not been too charming a letter, but I wanted to write and tell you I adore you. Take care of T'Nookie and yourself. I love you both.

Until tomorrow then – your boy baby sends hugs & kisses.

Donnie

XXOOXXOOXX

By the time Donald was finishing up this two-part letter, the news had broken of Hitler's death, and this officer minced no words about how he felt about it. His loneliness was getting the best of him, as he imagined all the little things he was missing at home. Sadly, he wondered if his little girl would even know him when he finally returned.

On the warfront, the news in Europe looked rosy with the defeat of Germany. But there was still another enemy to contend with—Japan.

DE Storey, Lieut (jg) USN
USS Carbonero (SS 337)
c/o F.P.O., San Francisco, Cal.

Mrs. D.E. Storey
Mount Vernon
New York

Thursday Evening
May 3, 1945
At Sea
#10

My Darling Sweetheart –
I have been constantly wondering about you and T'Nook today. There are so many things I want to know about, and I can hardly wait to hear.

Afraid there's not much news from my end. My health is excellent, but my morale is low 'cause I miss you, angel. I miss you more than I ever have. We seem so much closer now than we did a year ago, and there are so darn many things I miss. Little things that would mean nothing to most people – things like washing your hair, tucking snook in, putting water in the furnace – I could go on for hours, but no doubt you too miss the same little things. There is one thing in particular that gets me – I don't like to sleep alone. I can turn over but no one turns with me. Remember how close we used to sleep – almost as one!

Friday Evening
May 4, 1945
at Sea

My Dearest Darling –

I got just so far last night when we were summoned for a night of drills and exercises. Little sleep was garnered by all hands, mainly Don. However, I managed to snatch a few winks this morning, and that plus a shower makes me feel like a million bucks.

Darling, I haven't written every day but I can honestly say I've written every chance I have had. So far this trip has turned out to be quite strenuous.

Darling, I miss you too darn much. Honest, when I'm on the bridge for four hours I find I can think about and concentrate on one subject and one alone. That subject is always you.

Looks like the war in Europe will be over in a matter of days. It will be wonderful news to receive. Do you really believe Hitler is dead? Somehow I don't quite think so. I hope not, as death is too good for him – he should die a slow death by torture. See, angel, I have a personal grudge against Adolf as he is the one who is keeping us apart by starting this maelstrom.

Does T'Nook still know my picture? Tell the little cutie she had better remember her daddie or there will be one heart with a crack in it. Afraid she couldn't break it, as you, my darling, are the one who owns my heart.

I still haven't finished "Forever Amber"! I am sort of glad to read it in phases, as it too holds a lot of wonderful memories. Remember how engrossed we became in the book – that was the cause of many a burned potato. How I wish I could smell them burning right now.

Guess your allotment is in the bank by now.* Must feel good to know you at least have a nickel. We couldn't have lasted too much longer at the LaConcha** – particularly with those one armed bandits robbing us night after night. If there had been more time, however we could have stayed together if it involved begging, borrowing, or stealing. I'll never forget the fight we had over money in Newport, and it will never happen again. Guess I was just an old stinker.

Darling, I wish I could find the words to express how much I miss you and T'Nook. Nothing seems to give the full meaning of the way I feel. I just miss, I guess.

I worship you and love you with all my heart.

Donnie

P.S. Equal shares for you and T'Nook

XXXXXXXXXXXXXXXXXXXXXXXX

---

*A married serviceman was expected to allot $22 of his pay each month to his wife. The Government matched it with an additional $28. The allotment went up if the serviceman had children, so in addition to Donald's contribution, Mardy was receiving $40 a month from the government for her and their child.[2]

**Donald was most likely referring to the LaConcha Hotel in Key West, Florida, presumably where he and Mardy spent evenings together during their time on the island. The historic hotel is still in operation.[3]

In this letter, Donald imagined an idyllic future with Mardy and his little girl. Although he was happy about his new assignment aboard the submarine, the gnawing need to be home with his family got the better of him. He was about ready to throw in the towel.

DE Storey, Lieut (jg) USN
USS Carbonero (SS 337)
c/o F.P.O., San Francisco, Cal.

Mrs. D.E. Storey
Mount Vernon
New York

Saturday Evening
May 5, 1945
at Sea
#11

My Adorable Darling –
How does tonight find you, my love? I wonder if you miss me tonight as much as I miss you. Every time I turn around something hits me right between the eyes and reminds me of some little thing we've done together. T'ain't fair, angel.

The last few days have been rather cool, and the leather jacket your mom and dad gave me a year ago Christmas has come in mighty handy. Spent this afternoon squaring away some much neglected paperwork – one job you know I like! Everything is ship shape for a time at least. Today was the skipper's birthday, and he sported his new lounging robe to breakfast. Remember when you gals went to Hartford* after the bathrobes?

I just came off watch. Very beautiful sunset and clear as a bell. Just a bit on the chilly side however. Hope you are starting to have some warm weather. Sure would like to see T'Nook in a swimsuit. I just undressed and am now wearing the bathrobe you bought for me. Feel real civilized, but definitely don't feel at home – there never will be a time I'll feel at home without you around.

Darling, I have already reached the familiar point of wanting to resign from the Navy. I just can't take being away from you. Thoughts of that little cottage by the side of the road where we can watch the rest of the world go by are mighty appealing. Not that I don't like submarines. I definitely do – far more so than I did destroyer duty. This really is the prize duty – sea duty I mean – the Navy has to offer. There is a feeling of camaraderie and confidence that you find seldom, if not at all, in surface ships. All in all, I'm damn glad I changed, more so because of our wonderful 10 months together than anything else, naturally.

How is little T'Nookie? I think I have shown her picture to everyone on the Carbonero, and I have yet to hear anything but compliments. However, they all say she must owe her looks to her mother – with which I heartily agree.

Darling, don't forget you promised me you would go to Bachrach** and have a picture taken. No excuses, beautiful, just send a picture! Tough, ain't I!

Sweetheart, I wish tonight were a party night. Perhaps in our dreams we will have one. Just to hold you in my arms and feel that warmth run through my veins. Here I go again torturing myself and you as well.

With that, my darling, I will say good night. My thoughts and love are with you and T 'Nook now and always.

I'll Adore You Forever,

Donnie

XXXXX

---

*The capital of Connecticut.

**Bachrach was a chain of famous portrait photo studios.[4]

While waiting to send and receive mail, Donald continued to be faithful with his letters. Here, he recounted the day's news aboard ship, and gave a glimpse into the personalities of a couple of his crewmates. He also painted a colorful picture of his exuberant visits to Mardy at her house in Mount Vernon. And, he most certainly wasn't letting up when it came to nagging his wife about getting her driver's license!

DE Storey, Lieut (jg) USN
USS Carbonero (SS 337)
c/o F.P.O., San Francisco, Cal.

Mrs. D.E. Storey
Mount Vernon
New York

Sunday Evening
May 6, 1945
at Sea
#12

My Dearest Darling –
Here we are at the end of another week – many many miles apart but together in our thoughts and dreams. No matter how far or how long we may be apart, we will always be together in our hearts. Darling, before I proceed any further I just want to say "I love you."

Today was just another day. I had the 4–8 watch this morning, but the time got all mixed up some way or another and I benefitted by an extra hours sleep while Larry had a 5 hour watch. The day went quickly, and before I knew it I was back on watch again for four hours. I just came off, and am now sitting at the desk with my bathrobe and loafers on writing to the one I love above all else in the world.

Expect I'll be able to mail all my letters in three or four days. Hope also to be on the receiving end of a goodly number – if not I'll be heartbroken and you will hear my cries of anguish all the way across the blue Pacific. Gosh how I'm looking forward to hearing from you and T'Nook.

Everything is going along nicely. The Skipper jumped all over George tonight about something, and he's feeling sort of low. I tried to cheer him up, and think I did some good. Thus far, he has never bawled me out but there will undoubtedly come a day. I just finished talking to the "Shadow". That boy is quite a character, but he has an infectious sense of humor and you can't help but like him.

How is the Beast? Have you made any progress towards acquiring a driver's license? You had better have one before I get home! Guess in a month or two when we're out of debt to our parents you can have the Beast spring cleaned. I was just reminiscing this morning about how I used to pull into the street of 100 dogs, jump out of our puddle jumper, vault the porch railing, and plant a big smacker on Mardets. Remember the two or three times I forgot the last – I'll never forget! I've told you time and again you married a no good. No good or whatever I am, there is one thing I do know – I love you with all my heart.

Until tomorrow, adorable one, I'll say goodnight to you and T'Nook.
Forever Yours, With Hugs and Kisses –
Donnie
XXXXXXXXXXXXXOOOOOOO

On May 7, 1945, Germany officially surrendered to the Allies. The unconditional surrender took effect the following day, known as V-E (Victory in
Europe) Day.[5] Donald awkwardly tried to explain how he felt about the news,
perhaps not really meaning what he wrote. Nevertheless, what surfaced in this
letter was some resentfulness. While others were able to go home, the end of
his service was nowhere in sight.

DE Storey, Lieut (jg) USN
USS Carbonero (SS 337)
c/o F.P.O., San Francisco, Cal.

Mrs. D.E. Storey
Mount Vernon
New York

Monday Evening
May 7, 1945
at Sea
#13

My Dearest Darling –
How did you like the good news? There are probably many happy people
in the world today. I'll bet it won't be long now before you and I can celebrate a victory day. It may seem strange, and perhaps unpatriotic, but that
war has never meant much to me – it never seemed like my war, consequently today was just another day. Sounds callous no doubt, and what I'm
really trying to say is I want to come home and I'm jealous of all those guys
in the European Theatre who will be doing just that. Gosh, what's it going
to feel like after we've been apart for three or four months.

Today was spent making preparations for entering port – cleaning up,
catching up on reports, paperwork etc. Just a few more days and we'll both
be receiving letters. Yippee! I had the 04–08 this morning and again this
evening. That's the best watch of the lot as you get both darkness and day-
light during the watch – sunset and sunrise I should say.

What did you and T'Nook do today? You both probably got up around 8 o'clock – I'm generous tonight – had breakfast and then T'Nook had a bath and nap while you and Gram had another cup of coffee, a cigarette, and a talk. Bet I'm right so far! After that it's anybody's guess!

Darling, I heard a song tonight that really expressed the way I feel. "Every Time We Say Goodbye I Die a Little" – Well, I didn't die, but I did leave my heart behind. It will always be with you.

My adorable one, if you will pardon the brevity of this epistle of my love for you, I am going to hit the sack – all alone and lonely without my "snookie puddin" to keep me comfy. I love you, darling.

Forever and Ever, Darling

Donnie

Screwy letter, is it not?

Your Lover

On V-E Day, millions of people all over the world took to the streets to cel-ebrate, but it was obvious to Donald that the men aboard the submarine *Carbonero* weren't going anywhere just yet—not while the fighting with Japan continued in the Pacific. Against this backdrop, he wrote the following letter.

DE Storey, Lieut (jg) USN
USS Carbonero (SS 337)
c/o F.P.O., San Francisco, Cal.

Mrs. D.E. Storey
Mount Vernon
New York

Tuesday Evening
May 8, 1945
at Sea
#14

My Adorable Darling –
I am so sleepy tonight that I don't know just how far I will get with this missle of love before my eyes close and I slip off into the wonderful land of dreams with you by my side.

The weather was quite a bit warmer today, and I really enjoyed my eve-ning watch – a warm sun and a gorgeous sunset. How was V-E day in Mount Vernon? I've been wondering just how much celebration went on at home today. Seems as if I'm always at sea when something happens which calls for a celebration. The last big news – invasion of Normandy* – caught me on my way to you. Wish this had found me in a similar situation.

Nothing much happened today, but somehow or other it passed rather swiftly. Of course one day away from you passes just about at the same rate as one week with you – it seems just about that way. Looking back, our 10 months together sure went by in one hell of a hurry. They were the 10 most wonderful months of my life, and in the days to come you can be sure I'll relive and cherish every moment of every day spent with you. As a matter of fact, it has only been four weeks and already I'm living in the past and dreaming of the future. That's just about the way it is.

Has T'Nook got her crib yet? She will probably be much more comfortable when she does. The little sweetheart was getting too big for her bassinet the last time I saw her, so I imagine she really is in need of a crib by now. I'll bet she has been sleeping with her mommie quite frequently. I know she has if "mommie" has felt as lonely in bed as "daddie" has. We'll never have double beds will we angel? I sleep so much better with you up close. We both curve at the right places for each other or something. Nuts ain't I!

Darling, that sand man is fast overcoming my reluctance to say goodnight. So, until tomorrow, sweets, tell T'Nook I love her. Give my love to Gram, Judy, and Ernie. To you, my dearest, I send all my love and devotion forever.

Always Your Best Beau,

Donnie

XXXXXXX

---

*On June 6, 1944, (D-Day), U.S., Canadian, and British troops landed on five Nazi-occupied beaches in Normandy, France, setting in motion the Allied invasion and subsequent liberation of Western Europe.[6]

The *Carbonero* was almost in port, and Donald was very excited to soon have a package of mail from Mardy. He was also wondering whether she and the baby had received their presents. Despite looking forward to seeing some of his friends, he still couldn't get over the fact that what he really wanted—to be home in Mardy's arms—was way beyond his reach.

DE Storey, Lieut (jg) USN
USS Carbonero (SS 337)
c/o F.P.O., San Francisco, Cal.

Mrs. D.E. Storey
Mount Vernon
New York

Wednesday Evening
May 9, 1945
at Sea
#15

My Beloved –
Tomorrow will be mail day, and I can hardly bide my time until I rip open the envelope of the first letter. No kidding, I'm ready, willing, and able to receive letters. Seems as if it has been ages, and then I glance at a calendar and realize that but four weeks have passed!!

Today was routine with the exception of a very very thorough inspection by El Capitaine. My compartments looked fairly good. Afraid there was some room for improvement.

Darling, has the package arrived? I hope nothing was lost or broken. Also hope you like the pocketbook. I didn't know just what size or type to buy, but this one looked good to my eyes. T'Nook probably won't get too much of a bang out of her doll, but that's all I could find. It is original to say the least.

Sure would like to bump into the King sometime within the next week or two. Bet he hasn't changed one bit. Expect I'll see plenty of fellows I haven't seen in some time – sounds cheesy but I want to come home! First time I've ever been homesick in my life.

Darling, this hasn't been much of a letter, but I just wanted to say again tonight that I love you. Tomorrow night I will have plenty of questions to answer and ask – I hope. So until then, angel, I love you and miss you with all my heart.

Forever Yours,

Donnie

P.S. Give T'Nook a big smacker

As he expected, Donald received a stack of letters from Mardy when the *Carbonero* arrived at Pearl Harbor. She had numbered each one, so he could read them in order. In the letter below, Donald responded to numbers one through eight in the batch. He must have been very excited, because his own letter numbering was incorrect, as he repeated the number 15 in this message. This error threw off his forthcoming letters. He also mistakenly put down April as the month, when he should have written May.

DE Storey, Lieut (jg) USN
USS Carbonero (SS 337)
c/o F.P.O., San Francisco, Cal.

Mrs. D.E. Storey
Mount Vernon
New York

Friday Evening
April 11, 1945
In Port
#15

My Dearest Darling –
Yesterday certainly was a wonderful day. I received twenty three of your letters, every one of which was read eagerly and earmarked for many many further readings. Darling, you can't imagine what it means to have a wonderful gal like you for a wife. I certainly am in love with you.

There was so much information for discussion in your letters that I don't quite know where to start. Suppose I start by telling you all about me and the news I know, and then I'll start answering each of your individual letters.

To begin with, we pulled in yesterday afternoon and with the gangway came a very large sack of mail. Your letters, along with those of Mother, Dad, and Gram were all tied in a bundle – the prettiest bundle I've ever seen. I immediately sat down and started reading, but due to continual interruptions it was after 3 o'clock before I had read them all. Then we went to a conference which lasted until 6 o'clock, after which we proceeded to have a few drinks. Al, Bill and I then got a hotel room and went to bed. Today I had to go to school, so I hadn't been on the boat from 4 o'clock yesterday afternoon until I returned at 5 this afternoon. The above is why I didn't have a chance to write last night.

Darling, I love you.

To continue. I saw B.B. S. and Chips at the Officer's Club, and also some other members of my class I don't believe you know. B.B. and Chips both asked me to send T'Nook and Mardy their love. Everything has been very hectic yesterday and today, but it is starting to settle down somewhat now. There were about 40 people waiting to see me when I came aboard this evening, and right now – 11:15 – is the first minute I've had to sit down and be alone with my two gals. George and I both go to school again from 8–4 tomorrow and the next day. More fun!

Now to return to your letters. In regards to #1, that certainly was one rugged day for you, darling, and I gave a sigh of relief when it was over and you were ready for bed. Of course, at that point I hadn't read #2 and heard about your sailor friend. Wish I had been there! In regard to #3, you tell that cute little minx who calls herself T'Nook that she had better never be on report again for heckling her beautiful mommie while she is writing to me. Darling, I wish I could see the two of you right now. I can close my eyes and there you both are, but it just ain't as satisfying as the real thing. Glad to hear our stuff finally arrived, and I'll bet T'Nookie was glad to see it. Did anything get lost or broken?

I think it was a grand idea for you and Mac* to stay together for those two days. It helped you both over a few rough spots. I honestly believe that the first few days are the toughest. None of them are very good when we are apart, but after the first couple of days it's a little easier to pull in your tummy, crack your lips into a smile, and hold on tight. Wish I could hold on tight to you for a few minutes tonight!

I am now on letter #6 where the weather was cold, drizzly, and just right for cuddling. Well, sweet heart, tonight is warm and clear but so help me Hannah it sure is just right for cuddling with you. A night never passes that isn't just right! No angel, there is nothing I can think of offhand that you can send me. Just keep the old letters and some more wonderful pictures coming my way. Your letters are all I really need.

In letter #7, you certainly made me feel like a proud father. It feels so darn good to know T'Nook knows what I look like. I sort of like that little stinker. She sure is getting to be a big girl, and I am very grateful to her for being such a big help to her mommie's morale. Aren't we two lucky people? You and I have what the rest of the world seeks for.

Darling, you are a very adorable person. I don't know just why Lady Luck was so very generous to me, but I do know she helped me win everything I'll ever want from life. You and T'Nook are my whole life, and I love my life.

You are not telling me a thing when you say T'Nook is cuter than other babies. She is without a doubt the prettiest and the best behaved baby it has ever been anybody's good fortune to observe. I'm not very proud of her – not much!

Dearest, I've reached #8, and I'm afraid that is where I must say good night. I really have to drop Mother and Dad a line, and as there are only 5 hours between now and getting up time I had better do just that and hit the hay.

I love you, my darling, and wish, just as you, that we could cuddle and sleep close not just tonight but every night. Sweet dreams, darling, and take good care of yourself.

I'll Love You Forever.

Donnie

XXXXXX

---

*Presumably a friend.

While in Pearl Harbor, the *Carbonero's* crew members were preparing for their first war patrol. Donald spent a lot of his time in training before they set off again. Although combat was underway elsewhere, for Donald, military life in Hawaii was rather uneventful. His letters, a blend of everyday news and ever sweeter expressions of love, continued to be a constant in Mardy's life.

DE Storey, Lieut (jg) USN
USS Carbonero (SS 337)
c/o F.P.O., San Francisco, Cal.

Mrs. D.E. Storey
Mount Vernon
New York

Saturday Evening
May 12, 1945
In Port
#16

My Dearest Darling –
A wonderful surprise in the form of four more letters from you awaited me when I returned from school this afternoon. Your letters certainly are wonderful, just like their originator.

I rose at 6 this morning and spent another day being a school boy. Had one beer after school and came back to the boat where I proceeded to lose all my money playing poker – silly lad that I am. Now I'll have to wait until payday to buy you and T'Nook tokens of my affection.

So T'Nook has a boy friend. Tell him not to get serious until I am introduced to the young gentleman. Can you imagine our T'Nook having a boy friend. I guess we are just a couple of old married people, and boy do I love it. Being married to you is the most wonderful vocation the world has to offer.

Darling, I am especially lonely tonight. I want to climb in bed with you and push your hair off your neck so I can put my head right there. Won't it be wonderful when we can spend each and every night together living the life we both love. Wasn't it fun to go to bed early, read, etc. I think those nights were just about my favorites. Just plain lazy!

Well, darling, it's past my bedtime and I have school again tomorrow. For tonight then, sweet dreams sweetheart. Give T'Nook a big hug and kiss. I love you, darling, with all my heart.

Forever Yours,

Donnie

Donald reveled in Mardy's letters filled with news about home and their baby, but they also stirred up the intense longing he felt for her. An innocent night out was a temporary distraction. He could only make do by hoping to see her in his dreams.

Mardy must have been delighted to know that Donald had received more of her letters. Though delayed, his responses to them eased her mind and gave her comfort. Even though she had the support of her family, and had their child by her side, their prolonged separation had to be as difficult for her as it was for him.

As Donald concluded this love note, he got a tad naughty!

DE Storey, Lieut (jg) USN
USS Carbonero (SS 337)
c/o F.P.O., San Francisco, Cal.

Mrs. D.E. Storey
Mount Vernon
New York

Tuesday Evening
15 May, 1945
In Port
#18

My Beloved –
Received another of your wonderful letters tonight. It is so good to hear every detail about you and T'Nook. Wonder what you both are doing tonight? I have the duty, and expect I will make a trip to dreamland very early tonight. That is by far the best part of every day, as then I am always with you.

Last night, we attended a party given for submarine officers by request of the Skipper. He got a station wagon, and Jess, Al, Bill, Larry, and yours truly went along – decked out in whites, too! The Skipper picked up two girls he knows!! Afraid I didn't even make good conversation with them.

All in all, I had a nice evening, but it was mighty hard to crawl out at 5:30 this morning to get underway.

I was just looking through your letters and came across the picture of Judy and T'Nook. Honestly, darling, I hardly recognize her she has gotten so big. She looks so independent in that picture. It's very good, and I have it taped right at the head of my bunk along with the two pictures of you we took in Key West. My two gals – boy how I love 'em.

By now, you have probably received quite a few letters from me. It seems to take just five days for your letters to reach me. That really isn't too bad, Darling. I'll write every chance I have, as I know my letters mean as much to you as yours do to me.

You get your material for a new dress – them is orders from the Boss! Don't worry about trying to save, though I do think your idea of keeping a budget is a good one.

Angel, you talked of last June 15th. Wasn't that a gorgeous day?* Doesn't seem possible that practically a year has passed since then. We'll be old folks before we know it at this rate.

So you had the Carbonero napkin ring made into a bracelet.** Darling, I knew when you saw Mac's that you would want yours sooner or later. Glad you did have it done.

Darling, I talk to you every night just before I go to sleep. We usually have such nice talks. Just silly little things – once in awhile some serious subject creeps in. Then after we talk, we cuddle up real close. Some nights I can almost feel you – so soft, warm, and cuddly.

Darling, I'm so glad your bag is okay. I was worried for fear I hadn't picked out the right style. I was sort of impressed by the size of the Chanel bottle myself. Imagine that will last for a while? Did you find the penny in the pocketbook?

Dearest, I cannot comprehend ordering a bathing suit for T'Nookie. Where could you every find one small enough for her? Your idea about putting all our winter clothes together is darn good. That will make it lots easier when we set up housekeeping again.

Darling, buy yourself a pair of black panties with lots of lace. I'll probably never be allowed to see them on you anyhow – you old modest stinker!

You get yourself all outfitted with pants, slips, nightgowns, bras, etc. and then we'll just have a fashion show some night – just you and me.

After that reward, I think it is high time I said goodnight. I love you, my darling, and want you so much tonight. I want to press you close to me, run my hands along your back, and bite those tender ears. Darling, I adore you to pieces, and need you terribly.

Forever and Ever, a Heartfull of Love,

Donnie

XXXXXXXXXXXXXX (A million)

---

*June 15 was the day Donald left San Francisco for New London, Connecticut, to attend submarine school and reunite with Mardy.

**The bracelet was passed down to their daughter Marcy, who wears it to this day.

Donald was feeling positive about the war's inevitable end, and was in good spirits as he was continuing to receive Mardy's letters. But he was still waiting to receive the photo she promised him. In this letter, he mentioned their special song again: "As Time Goes By." With such an appropriate title, it seemed to take on even more meaning for him the longer they were apart.

DE Storey, Lieut (jg) USN
USS Carbonero (SS 337)
c/o F.P.O., San Francisco, Cal.

Mrs. D.E. Storey
Mount Vernon
New York

Wednesday Evening
16 May, 1945
In Port
#19

Hi Sweetheart –
Gee but I miss you tonight. I would like so much to be able to wash your hair (pour a little cold water on too!), help you take the clothes off the line, iron or most anything tonight. I just want to be where you are.

I received another of your super letters today. Darling, I certainly am a lucky fellow to have a "better half" who is so sweet, so beautiful, and just so scrumptious as you are.

The war news is looking better all the time. Don't believe the war will last much longer. We have an awful lot of power now. I know of two people who are going to be mighty happy when the last battle is won. How about it, darling?

The record that is playing is "I Guess I'll Have to Dream The Rest." That used to be one of our tunes. What memories songs can bring to the fore. Remember the night I sang "As Time Goes By" to you? We were sitting in the booth in the corner at the Pelham Pub. Darling, I was in love with you then, but that was a mere drop in the bucket compared to now.

Hey, when are you going to obtain your driver's license? Also, my love, what has happened to that nice glamorous photo Mr. Bachrach was going to take of the one I love? I'm not home to stomp on you, but I'll do it from here. I sure am one hell of a toughie!

Darling, my gunner's mate is paging me so I must be off.

With Love and Kisses I remain,

Yours Forever

Donnie

XXXXXXXXX

The hectic activities aboard the sub did not deter Donald from thinking more and more about his child. He wouldn't see her first developmental milestones, and this realization was no doubt very difficult for him.

DE Storey, Lieut (jg) USN
USS Carbonero (SS 337)
c/o F.P.O., San Francisco, Cal.

Mrs. D.E. Storey
Mount Vernon
New York

Thursday Evening
18 May, 1945
In Port
#20

My Darling –
This has been one busy day – some more underway training. Expect we will also have a busy night – not to mention the 12–4 watch I have. So, darling, if this letter comes to a sudden halt, you will know that work has commenced once again.

Due to the fact that we are underway tonight, I did not receive my sugar ration today, and I really do miss it. Your letters are scrumptious, and I can't help reading one that I don't feel happy and sad at the same time. The happiness is because you love me, and the sadness – need I say more! Someday – in the not too distant future – we will both know nothing but that happy feeling.

By now, you should have received the letters I wrote at sea. I wonder if they will all come in a bunch. Wish there was some say of arranging it so you received a letter a day instead of the entire caboodle at once.

How is little snookie? Does she really say "Da Da"? What I wouldn't give to see you both tonight. Guess she will be walking before long. Doesn't seem possible that two years ago we were looking forward to June week! We weren't even officially engaged, and now look at me! "Life Can Be

Beautiful". "Sweetie Face" just poked his head in and said to give you and snooks his best. He and the captain are hitting it off much better these days. As a matter of fact, all is peace and quiet in the wardroom country.

Last night after I finished dropping you a note, George and I took a bottle of liquor and went over to B.O.Q.* We sat around in a vacant room and talked and drank until midnight. Consequently, when 5:30 rolled around this morning I was in no mood to get up. But mood or not, I got up!

Oh oh, the call to duty has arrived. Until tomorrow then I'll sign off with a heart full of love to you both.

Your Ardent Admirer and Lover,

Donnie

XXXXXXXXXXXXXXXXXXXXXX

---

*Bachelor Officer Quarters.

Exhausted from training, Donald took advantage of an opportunity to go ashore, wash up, and relax. Clues in this letter and a subsequent one suggest Mardy may have known he was in Pearl Harbor.

DE Storey, Lieut (jg) USN
USS Carbonero (SS 337)
c/o F.P.O., San Francisco, Cal.

Mrs. D.E. Storey
Mount Vernon
New York

Friday Evening
19 May, 1945
In Port
#21

My Sweetheart –
I love you, I love you, I love you. What could be a more appropriate begin-ning to a letter to the most adorable "snookie puddin" in the whole wide world. I sure was disappointed tonight when the mail came aboard and not a single letter for yours truly. Perhaps tomorrow will be a better day.

I brought the boat in this afternoon, and made a darn fine landing if I do say so myself. Ahem! Yes, my cap will still fit the next time I see you. You are the direct cause of everything good I do. Believe it or not (by Donnie) ever since I married you I seem to have gained a tremendous amount of self confidence. Here I go letting my hair down again! I couldn't ever drop the ball with you as my right arm. Darling, I love you so much I could hug you until I didn't have one ounce of strength left in my torso. Would I like to do that right now!

George and I went up to B.O.Q. tonight and took showers. After we were sweet and clean we played one game of pool, went to the movies on board the good ship Carbonero, and here I be now writing to my O.A.O. I'm sitting here with nary a stitch on except my striped skivvie pants, drinking a glass of tomato juice and wishing you and I were going to have a whale of a party.

The last two days were long and tedious, and I can't say I was sorry to see them end. Only trouble is we have more of the same next week.

Tomorrow, I am planning to go in town and buy you and "little snook" a present or two. If I sent you grass skirts would you put on a show for me when we are all together again?

Well, darling, the sandman is after me again. Off to dreamland and you – a trip I love.

Forever Yours, with Love & Kisses,

Donnie

XXXXXXX

OOOOOOOO

XXXXX

DE Storey, Lieut (jg) USN
USS Carbonero
c/o F.P.O., San Francisco, Cal.

Mrs. D.E. Storey
Mount Vernon
New York

Tuesday Evening
22 May, 1945
In Port

My Dearest Darling –
Here I be after a one day lapse – a long, tiring, eventful day in which I couldn't find one minute to write to the one I love.

Tonight finds me at the Royal with a great big room all to myself. George has an adjourning room. We came in to have a real good night's rest, but as luck would have it I ran across an old Mt. Vernon friend, so it is not so early now. I was walking through the gardens after dinner when who should I bump into but Les J. Don't know whether or not you recall him, but he was quite an athlete while we were in hi-school. Anyhow, I luckily had a good bottle of stateside whiskey in the room which I picked up in Panama, so he and his two marine buddies came up to the room and we drank the liquor and had a bull session. They are all marine sergeants and have just returned from Iwo Jima. What stories those boys can tell! The three of them are here on a five day pass.

As yet, I still haven't received a letter from you saying you've received my letters. Your letters have been wonderful, and I could squeeze you to pieces for some of the things you have said in them. You always say everything I want to hear.

Well, my good night's rest is almost shot so if you'll excuse me I'll beg off for now. Lots to follow tomorrow.

I love you, dearest, with every breath in my body.

Forever and Ever (x 1 trillion)

Donnie

Toward the end of the month, Donald was still in port, and still on the hunt for gifts for his two girls. His time in Pearl Harbor, however, was drawing to a close. The following letter was the last one written in May 1945 to survive.

DE Storey, Lieut (jg) USN
USS Carbonero (SS 337)
c/o F.P.O., San Francisco, Cal.

Mrs. D.E. Storey
Mount Vernon
New York

Wednesday Evening
May 23, 1945
In Port
#24

My Darling –
Good evening, love of my life. Wonder what you and little Miss Storey are doing tonight. Perhaps you are both doing the same as I – dreaming and thinking of those you love.

This morning I awoke around 8:00, had a fine breakfast, and then went shopping for my two gals. Hope you both like what I found. Darling, the package was wrapped up for mailing in the store; consequently I was not able to enclose a card. In lieu of the card let me say that the package is for my two favorite people with every bit of love, devotion, and adoration I possess. I think I had the right sizes – however, T'Nook's things may be a bit too large.

I had letters from Mother and Dad today, and they are certainly anxiously awaiting you and T'Nook. Guess they have a room all fixed up for their grandchild. They are darn cute. Everyone says you look wonderful. I think you always did and always will look wonderful, so they aren't telling me a thing.

Everything has been a big flail today for some reason. Lots of activity and little accomplished. I bought two more pair of khaki pants so I have plenty of them now. Remember the afternoon we traipsed all over New London picking up all shades, types, and sizes of pants? Didn't we used to have fun going marketing in the afternoon.* Honestly, angel, we have such a good time when we are together that I think it makes it so much harder for us to be apart than any other people I know. No other couple has the fun we have – especially over little things.

The next two days are going to be busy ones, so perhaps it is just as well I write to the one I love and turn in. Not a minute of the day passes that I don't think of you and wish I were where you are, doing what you are doing. I'm over ready to wash a dish, change a diaper, lock a door – what I really mean is I'm ready to come home to my two beautiful ladies. This is one period of our lives I don't want time to stand still. Hurry up days and pass by so I'll be with my Mardy and little T'Nook.

Goodnight, Dearest, I love you now and Forever,

Donnie

XXXXXXXXXXX

There is a reason why Donald put all the stamps upside-down on his envelopes. It was a code meaning "I love you." (William Cochrane, "The Language of Stamps," The Philatelic Database, May 1, 2013, http:// www.philatelicdatabase.com/nostalgia/the-language-of-stamps.)

---

*This occurred when Donald and Mardy were living together while he was training at the submarine base in New London, Connecticut.

Donald and Mardy dressed for a dance when he was a midshipman at the United States Naval Academy in Annapolis, Maryland and Mardy was attending Mary Washington College.

All photos courtesy of the Storey family, unless otherwise noted.

Mardy's dance card from one of her dates with Donald.

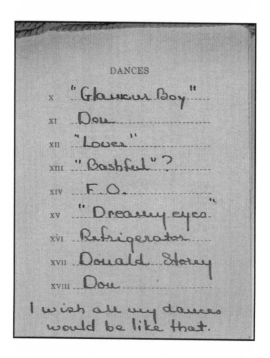

Donald in his Navy uniform.

Mardy on her wedding day.

Donald and Mardy on one of their rare visits.

Mardy's Backrach portrait.

Mardy with the couple's baby, Margery (Marcy).

Donald with little Margery.

Mardy working as a stenographer for Texaco.

This image appeared in the Spring 1944 issue of *The Texaco Star*.

Photo taken by R. I. Nesmith and provided by the Chevron Heritage Center.

Donald and Mardy later in life.

Don Jr. and Vicky Storey with Mardy, taken in 2014 in
New York during my visit to meet them.

Photo by Lisa Franco

Donald and Mardy's children, (L-R) Don Jr., Marcy, and Chris,
taken at Mardy's committal service in 2018 on Cape Cod.

Photo by Lisa Franco

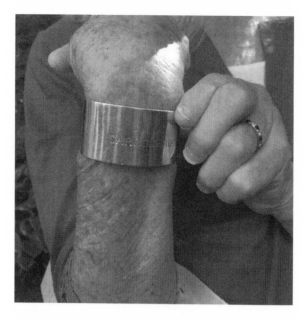

Marcy Waters wearing her mother's bracelet made from a USS Carbonero napkin ring.

Photo by Lisa Franco

CHAPTER ELEVEN

War Patrol

The USS *Carbonero* left Pearl Harbor on May 26, 1945, for her first war patrol. She mostly remained on lifeguard duty off the island of Taiwan on the Chinese coast.[1] This involved standing by to rescue U.S. airmen in the water after their planes were struck down by the enemy.[2]

As June progressed, Donald became more and more torn between his duty to his country and wanting to be with Mardy and their child. He would celebrate his first Father's Day at sea—a sacrifice many young servicemen make to this day—lost time and lost memories, never to be recovered.

[No address information available]

Saturday Evening
June 9, 1945
at Sea
#38

My Dearest Darling –

How's everything tonight, angel? Hope you are not as warm as I am at the present moment. Darling, I didn't write last night because of fatigue, but I know you'll excuse when I tell you how much I love you. Honestly, darling, I love you so very very much it hurts.

Tomorrow, being Father's Day, I'll get to read my cards from you and T'Nook. Wasn't I a good boy to wait like you both told me to?

My poor old kisser has really been taking a beating lately. Finally, in desperation, I wore a handkerchief over my face today and looked like the "masked marvel". At any rate, it served its purpose and my face is not like a raw piece of steak tonight. The old sun is really terrific.

Wonder if my package has reached you as yet. I have an idea you will like the skirt, but about the blouse – I don't know. It is sort of flashy – but kinda purty too.

Well, darling, another letter must come to a close – one more day gone by. I love you with every breath I take. I want you by my side now and forever. You are everything I want in life.

Forever Yours,

Donnie

When Donald wrote the following letter, he was under the impression it was Father's Day, when in reality it wasn't for another week. Still, it was a bittersweet day. Despite being separated from his family, he considered himself a lucky man. The precious cards he had to read were his only connection to Mardy and the baby—otherwise, it was sea life as usual. Curious as to whether Mardy had gone for her driver's license, he continued to press her for information.

[No address information available]

Sunday Evening
June 10, 1945
at Sea
#39

My Precious Darling –

It seems strange to notice that today is Sunday. Can't say it much resembles our happy Sundays together – days in which we rarely did more than be alone, having good times in ways only you, I and T'Nook know. Thank you both so very much for the cards. I read them at 4:00 this morning after coming off watch, and then I dropped off to sleep secure in the knowledge that I am – without a single doubt – the luckiest person in the world. Tell Miss Snookie Storey that her Daddy thinks his card is the nuts.

I stood the mid watch again last night – my old standby – and as a result I slept in this morning until late. Another watch, some routing work, and here I am telling you I love you with all my heart.

By the way, beautiful, I learned a swell game last night which we can add to our repertoire. It is rather complicated and goes by the name "Cameroon". All one needs to become involved is ten dice and a glass. Remember our cribbage games?

Have you taken your driver's test as yet, angel? In one of your letters you mentioned making an appointment by mail, but as yet I haven't heard the results. I know you won't have any trouble.

T'Nook and I had a long talk last night, and we decided that you are just about the sweetest thing running around hereabouts. No kidding,

T'Nookie told me that you and she have a wonderful time together, but that you both miss me – makes me feel like a million dollars.

Dearest, dinner is on the table, so I'll bid you sweet dreams for another night. I love you, darling, more today than yesterday if such is possible.

Forever and Ever Yours

Donnie

After he realized his error about Father's Day, Donald admitted it in this good-humored letter. His sweet description of memories of their romance is another demonstration of how much Mardy meant to him, and how much he wanted to be with her, even though only two months had passed since he last saw her. He also was all too aware that in his absence their baby was getting bigger by the day.

[No address information available]

Tuesday Evening
June 12, 1945
at Sea
#40

My Dearest Darling –

Good evening, beautiful. How is the love of my life tonight? After all my bragging about being such a good boy and waiting until father's day before reading my cards, I was quite red in the face Sunday evening when I discovered that father's day is the 17th – not the 10th. Live and learn!

Sunday night I had a wonderful four hours on the bridge. I talked to you about our memories. Honestly, darling, when you look back to the very beginning – our first date – and start bringing it all up to date! Well, anyhow, at the end of four hours we still weren't married! What a host of beautiful memories. I ran the gauntlet of emotions – from tears to laughter. Perhaps this all sounds like I am going slightly batty – maybe I am – but the fact remains that I did have a wonderful time. I practically relived every date, every kiss, and every laugh. Some night when we both feel contented and comfortable in our own house – after T'Nook is sound asleep – I am going to take you in my arms and recapture last Sunday night – only with a real you to talk to.

How is our little bundle of sweetness. Bet she enjoys getting outside in the sun with next to nothing on. She has probably grown so fast in the past 2 ½ months that I wouldn't know her. I think I really would though, don't you?

Darling, it doesn't seem possible that only two months have passed since we said "so long for now". Every day away from you seems like a month. I love you, darling, with all my heart and would give anything to hold you close tonight and lay my head where it belongs.

All My Love Forever,

Donnie

Still torn between duty and family, Donald's mood was as gray as the weather. Most likely he kept this letter short to avoid upsetting Mardy.

[No address information available]

Wednesday Evening
June 13, 1945
At Sea
#41

My Beloved –

One more long, grey, rainy day gone by. I got soaked to the skin this afternoon, and was certainly glad to get below and into some dry clothes.

Tonight I feel rather tired and blue. Would like so very much to be with you. You are such a big part of me that at times I feel lost when I realize we are so far apart. It just seems a d– – – shame that all these days have to slip past with so little meaning in our lives. I know in my mind that my rightful place is out here as long as I am needed, but my heart sings a different tune. I need you and T'Nookie. My life could never be complete nor contented without you.

Guess I'm sort of crying on your shoulder tonight. Can't help it, beautiful. I just love you too much not to give voice to my feelings. Wish I could write a foolish, funny letter – but tonight just isn't the night. Mayhap tomorrow night I will be able to make you laugh a little.

So darling, with that thought in mind I will say goodnight to the one I adore with my mind, body and soul. Sweet dreams, sweetheart. I love you.

Donnie

Besides Mardy, little Margery continued to weigh heavily on Donald's mind. Starved for information, he remembered some of the sweet things she used to do during the short time he was with her, and wanted to know all about her latest developments.

The *Carbonero* was still off the coast of Taiwan,[3] and from the content of Donald's message, it appears as if the crew was not seeing a lot of action.

[No address information available]

Thursday Evening
June 21, 1945
at Sea
#44

My Beloved –

It is strange how time seems to draw us closer together. For the first month it seemed as if we were very far apart – perhaps the initial separation caused that – but now, darling, you seem much closer to me. Perhaps it is because I have missed you so darn much. Or maybe I'm a bit unbalanced. Whatever the cause, sometimes I feel as if you are so very near.

Today was a replica of many of those which have gone before it – a mid watch last night, late sleep this morning, dinner, afternoon watch, supper and now I'm writing to you – my favorite occupation. Darling, won't it be super if the day ever comes when we don't have to write one another ever again. I'm hoping we will always be so close that "whispering only" will be the rule.

How is T'Nook? There are so many questions about her which come to my mind during the day, and fly away as soon as I start writing. I want to ask all the little things – does she still sleep with her hands over her head?; does she still play with the Johnson's baby powder container?; can she drink out of a glass?; when did (or will) she start wearing shoes? I know that the answers to all these questions are in your letters, but the wait for them is an impatient one. Imagine that works for both ends!

Darling, looking back on our life together – I arrive at but one conclusion – it has been perfect. I couldn't ask for any more than I have. I have often kicked myself for some of the times I went "temperamental" on you and caused a spat. That, to me, is all part of the wonderful partnership and love we hold. Little quarrels seem to strengthen our marriage and weave our love closer to our hearts.

Darling, I don't know what has come over me lately. Such serious letters! I am trying to tell you how much I love you, but I certainly get all involved. So, for tonight, my love,

I Adore You,
Donnie

As June drew to a close, Donald's days on board the *Carbonero* continued to be steady, uneventful, and prolonged, save for some rough seas. His tedious routine only exacerbated his longing for his family. In this letter, he inquired about a major developmental stage in his daughter's life—another milestone he would not be around to witness.

[No address information available]

Wednesday Evening
June 27, 1945
at Sea
#48

My Dearest Darling –

The days drag on somehow, and I keep on missing and loving you like the very devil. Darling, why is it that you and I feel separations so much more than any other people we know? I am convinced, beyond a shadow of a doubt, that we have a much deeper and stronger love than most have.

The routine remains the same with little or no variation. What a difference from our life together! You probably feel the same way, but I imagine T'Nookie helps loads.

I feel differently this time than I did before. I am afraid I wouldn't be content to come home to you for a few days now. When I come home to you, or when you come to me I want it to be for all time. Not that a few days or even a few hours together wouldn't be wonderful! It would make everything just a little harder, though, don't you think?

The card playing cycle has now rolled around to bridge, and George and I really got taken over the hurdles last evening. At 1/10 cent a point too! That's where our bank roll goes!

The night before last I had an eclipse of the moon during my watch. First one I have ever seen, and it was kind of eerie. Last night was a wet one – rain and heavy seas. I looked like I'd been in swimming with all my clothes on when I came off watch at 4:00 this morning.

Darling, has T'Nook ever crawled or is she going to by-pass that stage and just start walking? That is one thing I really hate to miss – those first tottering unsteady steps. Can you imagine learning to walk?

Beautiful, once more I must close and get cleaned up for supper. I love you, my darling, and think of you every minute of every day. Be good girls and kiss one another for your old man.

Forever and Ever Yours,

Donnie

XXXXXXXXXXX

OOOOOOOOO

The *Carbonero* was nearing the end of her first war patrol, and Donald was looking forward to getting into port and receiving some long-awaited letters from Mardy. In this message, he professed to continue his letter writing and expressed more concern over finances, apologizing for spats they had in the past. His letter numbering slipped again, as he assigned this letter the same number as his previous one.

[No address information available]

Friday Evening
June 29, 1945
at Sea
#48

My Beloved –

At this very minute, I am sitting here listening to the Warsaw Concerto* – feeling very serious – and missing you beyond comprehension. Come on out and live with me, angel. How I wish you could. Won't be too long though, before that wonderful day when we can start living again.

Nothing out of the ordinary has happened these past two days. I got quite a sunburn today, but it is not painful. Just makes me look healthy. Guess both my gals are getting tanned these days also. Wouldn't it be super to be able to meet at the pool every afternoon like we did in Key West.

The days are rolling by. In a few weeks I'll start to meet the mailman. Can hardly wait. What a bunch of letters I will have this time! I'm doing my best to have plenty to send, but, darling, I'm getting very lazy. So far, however, I've been a pretty good boy about writing, and I know darn well I'll continue to be. Once I get started there is nothing I like more than writing to you.

The allotment check this month should just about wipe out our debts, shouldn't it? I mean with my parents, your parents, the mechanic who fixed the Beast etc. I'll never forgive myself for those petty quarrels we had over money – Newport for example. I guess I'm just a "worry wart", but I did so want you and T'Nook to be well taken care of that sometimes I was sort of touchy. Forgive me?

My lovely one, the time has come when I must bid you a fond adieu for this lonely night. I'll see you in my dreams – hold you close and kiss you behind that gorgeous left ear.

Goodnight –
Yours Forever,
Donnie
XXXXXX
OOOOOO

---

*"The Warsaw Concerto" was written in 1941 by British composer Richard Addinsell for the movie *Dangerous Moonlight*.[4]

CHAPTER TWELVE

Subic Bay

On July 8, 1945, The *Carbonero* completed her first war patrol and went on to be refitted at the U.S. Naval Base at Subic Bay, Philippines.[1] As was the case with all of the correspondence written in June, there were no surviving envelopes accompanying the first part of Donald's July letters. But according to an incomplete letter he wrote to Mardy on July 2, Donald planned to send some of his letters to the family lake retreat in upstate New York, where she would be vacationing for a while. Although Donald knew where Mardy was, she still could only guess his whereabouts.

In the following message, Donald remembered some antics he and Mardy would engage in after dinner each night, and alluded to some war activity aboard the *Carbonero* a couple of days prior. Back home, the baby was nearing a year old, and Mardy's sister Judy was preparing for college.

[No address information available]

Thursday Evening
July 5, 1945
at Sea
#50

My Dearest Darling –
How is the love of my life tonight? I'll bet you miss our fun after supper

every night as much as I do. Remember how you used to bump me against the sink, and how we used to chase each other around? What a couple of nuts!

A major calamity took place today. Remember the khaki cap I bought in Key West? I've worn it every day since, and it has really afforded my nose excellent protection. Well, this afternoon Mr. Wind took charge and over the side my beautiful cap did go. Al is the remaining person who has not suffered a similar fate. You should have heard the Skipper's language the day his went the way of all good caps!

The fourth of July was certainly tame. Not even a firecracker! Wonder what my beautiful wife and adorable daughter did to celebrate Independence Day?

Two days ago we had some fun, the details of which must wait until some later day. Not too much later either, I am hoping.

It won't be long before T'Nookie is 11 months old. Doesn't seem possible. In some ways it seems like only yesterday that I left you in the hospital and hopped the train back to New London. How I hated to leave you that night!

I imagine Judy is getting excited about entering Mary Washington in the fall. Too bad I don't know anyone at the Academy now, but imagining Judets will have little or no trouble on that score.

Darling, you are such a big part of me that it always seems as if something is missing. To hold you close once again and whisper "I love you"! Whew, that sends shivers up and down my spine just thinking about it. Darling, I love you from the tip of your toes to the top of your head. Right now I could eat you up – no foolin!

Good night "love bugs"! (both of you)
Your Ever Lovin Hubby and Daddy
Donnie

When Donald wrote this letter, he was one day away from arriving at Subic Bay[2] and very excited about getting his mail. But what he really wanted was for Mardy to be there when he got to port. It was a pipe dream, of course, and all he could do was rely on more of his wife's correspondence to help fill the rapidly expanding void within his heart.

[No address information available]

Saturday afternoon
July 7, 1945
at Sea

My Beloved Darling –
Tomorrow will be a gala day. Not only will I have a chance to send my letters on my way to you, but in all probability, I will have over a month's mail waiting for me.

The past two days have been long and crowded. The weather has been stinky to boot, but no more sea duty for a few weeks! I'm hoping like all get out that I will be able to send a cablegram, but I don't know for sure whether or not such service is available.

Darling, how I wish you were to be waiting for me tomorrow. How many times that thought has run through my noggin during these past 24 hours! I'd give so much to be looking forward to a few weeks with you.

Darling, until tomorrow then, when I will have a dearth of news to write about I'll sign off with all the love, hugs and kisses in the world to you and T'Nookie.

Yours Forever and Ever,
Donnie

While the sub was in port, Donald was consumed with reading a large batch of Mardy's letters and looked forward to even more. He seemed relieved he had a few weeks to rest and reset, and even got into a little bit of trouble!

[No address information available]

Tuesday Morning
July 10, 1945
In Port

My Dearest Darling –

How wonderful the past few days have been. To date I have received 35 letters from you, all of them as full of news and words I love to hear that I hardly know where to begin.

At present we are in rest camp. Accommodations are simple and rough, but it is great to get away from it all for a while. Gosh, I have so much to tell you I hardly know where to begin.

The first night in – night before last to be exact – we had a drunken brawl. Every officer aboard the Carbonero was asleep by 6:30. Bunch of heavy drinkers! Your ardent admirer really couldn't take it.

I bought a wristwatch yesterday for $25. It's a Lucerne and really is a good looking watch. I won $12 playing poker last night, so that helped pay for the watch.

Darling, I'm afraid this is one place I won't be able to get a charm for you. I'm going to try and find one, but pickings don't look too good.

It sounds as if T'Nook is really getting to something. Glad to hear you and she received your package and that the dresses were the right size. Wish I could send you a package every day, but would really like to climb in a box myself and come to you by airmail.

There is not much to do here except sleep, eat, and drink. Al, Larry and myself went for a walk and a swim in a mountain stream this morning. We are going to take some pictures, and if they turn out at all I'll send you a set. I've really got quite a collection of T'Nook now, but how about some of my dream girl?

Gosh angel, how I wish I were going to be at the lake with you this summer. It's just a catastrophe.

Darling, I'll bet your new clothes are scrumptious. I want you to buy anything and everything you want, and I only wish I could take you out and buy out the town.

I'm so proud of T'Nookie and you. In every letter mother and dad say you both certainly make them proud that their son was fortunate enough to win such a lovely gal.

Just think, we have almost three weeks now to receive mail from one another. Your letters mean so darn much to me. Tonight I am going to write you another letter and start answering your letters. But now I just want to tell you how much I love you and want you near me. No matter what happens after the war – navy or civilian – Guam or Podunk – I am never going to let you out of my sight for more than a matter of hours.

We are all quartered in a Quonset hut and sleep on army cots. Have only had one opportunity to sample the food but that was pretty good. One thing we do have is a nice shower and all the water we want, which is really something after the length of time we have been to sea.

Darling, we've covered lots of miles since Key West, but I feel no farther away from you now than I did ten minutes after you left me on that horrible old bus. If anything I feel even closer now that the initial shock has worn off.

Well, loveable, it is time for lunch so I'll say goodbye for now. I'll write again tonight and every time I can get out of a horizontal position long enough to wake up.

I love you so very very much my darling, and would give anything to escort you to a great big old party right this minute.

Yours Forever,

Donnie

Although Donald was getting some much needed R & R, he would have much rather been with Mardy at the family retreat in upstate New York. It was during an earlier visit to the lake when the couple discovered how much they really cared for each other.

[No address information available]

Wednesday Morn
July 11, 1945
In Port

My Beloved Angel –
Well, darling, I fell asleep last night immediately after supper, and consequently the promised letter didn't get written. Guess I had too much exercise yesterday as I went swimming twice, hiked five miles, and played ping pong and horseshoes. My legs are sort of stiff today as a result.

It is really hot today. This is the rainy season, and there are oodles of bugs, but at least it is cooler here at this time of the year than at any other time.

My new watch seems to keep excellent time. Hope I don't lose it like I did the other one. I'll probably take it in swimming or do some other foolish thing. Your brilliant husband!

Sweetheart, why don't you come on out here and give me a big old kiss. I'll bet we could even sleep together in this great big hard army cot.

From your letters it sounds as if you, T'Nook and mother have been doing quite a bit of partying. Bet those parties weren't nearly as good as the ones we used to have (and will again).

Darling, I miss you and T'Nookie so very much. I know I repeat myself over and over again, but I have to tell somebody how much I hate this separation stuff. Even if it means hard times as a civvie, I'm not going to stand for times like this when the war is over.

One of your last letters speaks of a trip into the woods with mom after something or other, and you said you saw some poison ivy. I remember when that stuff really "took charge and marched off" just because I took you on a picnic.* Will you ever forget that train ride home? Gee but that seems like an age ago. I thought I loved you then, but I didn't even know what it is to love a person.

Haven't seen much of the Skipper since we came ashore as he lives in separate quarters and hob knobs with the big shots. I imagine he is glad to get away from all of us for a while.

So far we've had loads of fun doing nothing but gambling, sleeping, drinking, swimming, and eating. Lots of laughs at any rate. Right now some of the boys are playing darts. I'm not so hot at that.

Darling, I hope you have a lot of fun this summer. At least one hundred times a day I curse inwardly at this damn war when I think of the fun and happiness we could be enjoying at the lake. Remember the night we went for a canoe ride? We had a serious conversation, and I remember you saying that you were learning parts of my nature you'd never known before. Well, you know 'em all now. Poor gal!

Beautiful, I love you with every bone in my body. You're everything I've ever dreamed of, and I never want to let you out of my sight again.

Yours Forever,

Donnie

---

*According to their daughter Marcy, the reason why Mardy had long gloves on in her Naval Academy dance photo with Donald was because of this poison ivy incident!

In the following letter, Donald included a colorful description of a day trip he took, but his feelings of loneliness rose to the surface yet again. The lake had become so meaningful to him, and he couldn't stand the thought of his family being there without him.

He had become careless about numbering his letters, but he made a new attempt with this one.

[No address information available]

Thursday Afternoon
July 12, 1945
In Port
I'm going to start numbering all over again, OK?
#1

My Darling –
One more day closer to the time we start living and loving again. I received three more of your wonderful letters today, angel. Every time I read one I almost start swimming home, but I'm afraid I wouldn't make it, as it is one h– – – of a long way.

Yesterday was rather uneventful, though we did go over to a nearby village for a look see in the afternoon. What a mess! A real mud hole if I ever saw one! Pigs running around in the front yard (if you could call it that) and all that sort of thing. We were paddled across to the town by a native in an outrigger canoe. That was the only fun I had out of the whole trip.

I have all your letters I've received this time stacked neatly by number in front of me. In this letter or the next I'm going to start going through them and answering any questions. Most of them are probably already answered.

Darling, I'm in a blue mood today. Every time I turn around I think of you on the road to the lake, and I feel so darn lonely.

Beautiful, we used to get awful peeved about New London, but I would take it any time. We were together then, and that is all that matters. All I want out of life is to be with you. I love you so much that sometimes I feel like saying the h– – – with all the rest of the world and coming home to you.

I wonder what T'Nook will think of the lake. Someday, darling, we will have an entire summer there together. We will also have to spend a summer near salt water – for the benefit of my "angel pangel".

Well, darling, it's about time I hit the hay. Until tomorrow, I'll say good night and pleasant dreams. I love you with all my heart and soul.

Yours Forever and Ever,

Donnie

In this letter, Donald was looking forward to at last receiving a nice professional photo of Mardy. He was getting closer to finishing his notebook and earning his qualification in submarines. Still not able to disclose his location for fear of censorship, he dropped a little hint to start Mardy guessing.

It appears as if Mardy was very faithful with her letters to Donald, judging by their sheer volume. Although they no longer exist, some of their content is disclosed based on Donald's responses. This is how we learn that Mardy had her own personal achievement: finally getting her driver's license.

[No address information available]

Saturday Afternoon
July 14, 1945
In Port
#3

My Dearest Darling –
Two wonderful letters from you this morning! You are my life, my love, my everything.

One of your letters also had your appointment card for pictures by Bachrach enclosed. Please send the pictures by air-mail, or otherwise it will take months for me to receive them. I can't wait to see them, beautiful, and I do hope they turn out good.

I have just finished showering and shaving, and though I feel sweet and clean, I am damn hot. It must take a long while for one to get used to a tropical climate.

I received a letter from Judy this morning, and from the sound of it I would say she had a large crush on Warren F.'s son. She told me about her weekend at their place at Candlewood Lake.* Just wait until she meets the boys at the U. of Va! I certainly had a time competing with those jokers.

From what the Captain said today, it appears I'll get a chance to qualify after the next run. Guess I had better get on the ball and finish my notebook.

Darling, I just re-read some of your letters (41-50) to see if there are any questions I can answer. As I am now the recipient of #80 you can see how many letters I have received since we got in.

In one of your letters you mentioned my having some nice moments (in reference to where we were). Well, beautiful, perhaps I shouldn't say this (you'll get conceited), but I have not had one nice moment since I left you in Key West. Darling, there is nothing in the whole wide world that interests me when you're not around. Life is very very empty.

Another of your letters made my mouth water. You spoke of lettuce sandwiches. It has been a long time since I've had a nice fresh salad of any kind, and lettuce sure sounds yummy.

Darling, I'm afraid I've been so intent on telling you my troubles and attempting to tell you how much I love you, that until now I have not congratulated you on passing your driver's test. Now our insurance is good, and I just love you. Nuts, aren't I? I get all mixed up and inevitably nothing comes out but "I love you".

Darling, I only wish I could let you know where I am and where I'm going. All I can say is that I am in none of the places you have mentioned in your letters, and don't expect to see any of them for a while. I am near a place we've talked about often in regards to doing duty after war.

It's almost suppertime, and I am as hungry as a bear. If I get the opportunity I'll write again tonight. Gosh how I wish I could hug you and T'Nookie for a little while.

I love you so, sweetheart, and want you so very very much this evening. I'll never let you go once I get hold of you again.

Your Ardent Lover Forever (Whew!)

Donnie

---

*A lake in Connecticut.

[No address information available]

Sunday Eve
July 15, 1945
In Port
#4

Hello Sweetheart –

I could love you tonight until we both fell asleep from exhaustion. Fresh, am I not?

Today was not at all like Sunday. George and I went for a hike in the mountains this morning, and boy did your "old man" get hot and tired. I found out I'm not in tip top physical shape, as I had to stop and rest every fifteen minutes or so.

Spent this afternoon sleeping and playing poker, and I managed to recoup some of my losses. I took some pictures this morning, and as soon as I finish the roll, I'll try and find some means to have them developed and will send them on to the one I love.

It rained part of this afternoon, and when it rains out here it really rains. The other night my bunk was even flooded.

Darling, I went through some more of your letters tonight and I couldn't find any questions that I haven't already answered. Sounds as if you've really been collecting good things for our home – such as the NorthStar blanket, dish towels etc. That's the stuff, 'cause it won't be so long now before we settle down to some real living.

I doubt if I'll have a chance to write tomorrow, as George and I are going on a sightseeing trip, and probably will have to stay overnight.

I am enclosing some Jap money* to put in our scrapbook as a memento of the days we were both lonely and apart – days we will never repeat.

Well, darling, it's time for little Donnie to hit the hay. I love you, my darling, with all my heart and soul. Sweet dreams, sweetheart –

Forever Yours,

Donnie

*When Japan captured Pacific Rim territories, they confiscated all of the local currency and replaced it with their own Japanese invasion money (JIM). In the Philippines, it was in the form of centavo and peso notes. After Japan surrendered, the money was rendered even more worthless than it already was, and became souvenirs for servicemen to send home.[3]

After he returned from his sightseeing trip, Donald told Mardy about his activities. According to the envelope accompanying this letter, Mardy and the baby were staying at the Storey lake house by mid July.

In this letter, Donald talked about the inflated wartime prices in the Philippines. Considered cheap by today's standards, during this era Donald thought otherwise.

For privacy, the family's full address at the lake is not disclosed.

DE Storey, Lieut. (jg) USN
USS Carbonero (SS 337)
c/o F.P.O.
San Francisco, Calif.

Mrs. D.E. Storey
Checkered Rocks
New York
*c/o C.E. Storey Jr.**

Wednesday Evening
July 18, 1945
In Port
#5

My Beloved Darling –
It has been two days since I have had a chance to write. George and I had quite a trip, and though it was a wet and dirty two days, we saw some interesting sights. There is nothing left of what once must have been quite a beautiful city.** We "hob knobbed" with Commanders and Captains – the "Skipper" was along – and all in all had quite a good time. However, I was darn glad to get back to a shower and some clean clothes. Above all, there were seven wonderful letters from you, one from your dad, one from mother and one from Judy waiting for me.

The pictures of T'Nook are super. Golly but she has gotten big. You are so good at describing her tricks and everything, that I almost feel I'm right there watching her make "So Big" or watching her play peek-a-boo.

Bet you gals will have a wonderful "hen" party this summer, but I'll also wager that T'Nookie will be spoiled rotten. You know, I'm afraid I couldn't be like your Dad and mine. I just couldn't let you go away from me for the summer.

T'Nookie looks as if she has real curly hair. It will be wonderful if she does have natural curls.

Darling, enclosed is the nearest thing to a charm I have been able to find. There just aren't any wiggly ones to be had. The prices here are terrific. I wanted to buy a small ivory elephant to send you, but they wanted $25 for it. Can you imagine! Everything is that way - $1 for a bottle of soda pop - $1.25 for two fried eggs! I guess this is what you call inflation. Oh, angel, I have so much I'd like to tell you, but I must tuck it back in my memory section and bring it all forth some night when we're all alone in a place of our own.

Until the rest period is up, I intend to stay right near my bunk and my stationary, so prepare yourself for a deluge of crazy notes, sad missles, and love epistles. Boy, am I sharp as a tack tonight.

Darling, I love you so very very much. When I grab hold of you, I'm never going to let go. For the present, however, I must close my eyes and kiss you over and over again in my dreams.

Yours Forever (after that too!)

Donnie

P.S. Tale of woe:

I forgot to write mother on her birthday, so I'm going to write her and pre-date the letter the 12th. Help me smooth it over. Ain't I a "stinker" if there ever was one.

I love you,

Me

"Blue Eyes"

---

*Donald's father, Charles Edgar Storey.

**Donald was mostly likely referring to Olongapo City, near the Subic Bay Naval Station. Olongapo suffered major damage during the war.[4]

With the area still deluged by rain, Donald was biding his time sleeping and playing cards. He still had a couple of weeks before the *Carbonero* would pull out from Subic Bay and start her second war patrol.

As he mentioned in this letter, Donald was able to send a cablegram to Mardy. Unfortunately, it did not survive, so there is no way of knowing what news it contained.

DE Storey, Lieut. (jg) USN
USS Carbonero (SS 337)
c/o F.P.O.
San Francisco, Calif.

Mrs. D.E. Storey
Checkered Rocks
New York
c/o C.E. Storey Jr.

Saturday Evening
July 21, 1945
In Port
#8

My Beloved Darling –
Received your wonderful letter today telling me that you received the cablegram. That really is wonderful service. One day to go halfway round the world. Wish I could send you one every day, darling. I also received a letter from Gram with some grand pictures of T'Nook enclosed. She certainly looked darling, and what a poser!

I spent today doing practically nothing. Slept most of the morning, and played poker all afternoon. Won about $30 too. All in all this has been a lucky day. Of course we had our usual rain – nearly flooded us out.

Darling, Saturday night really is the loneliest night in the week. I am so proud of my two gals. Without a doubt, I have the two most beautiful "lover babies" in the whole wide world.

Right now I am sitting here drinking a bottle of Ruppert's beer, smoking a cigarette, and writing to the one I love above all else on this world or any other. We only have a few days of rest camp left, but I still have at least two weeks to write and mail my "love missles".

Darling, it will certainly be the happiest day in my life when this war is over and I know you and I will never be separated again for long periods of time. Sometimes I feel absolutely empty inside. Neither of us would have thought three years ago that such a love could be possible. I don't believe any other two people in the world really know what love is.

I love you so very much,

Donnie

At the time Donald wrote this next message, he had received more letters from Mardy, who had documented her trip to and arrival at the family lake retreat. It was likely the first time their daughter experienced the lake, and Donald had to miss it. His R & R at Subic Bay had come to an end, but as usual, his primary thoughts focused on romance, and holding Mardy in his arms.

DE Storey, Lieut. (jg) USN
USS Carbonero (SS 337)
c/o F.P.O.
San Francisco, Calif.

Mrs. D.E. Storey
Checkered Rocks
New York
c/o C.E. Storey Jr.

Monday Evening
July 23, 1945
In Port
#11

My Dearest Darling –
Today was another gala day as I received two letters from my snookie – one written on the way to the lake and the other just after you had arrived. Sounded like quite a lively trip what with relieving the watch on T'Nook and taking her in the boat for the first time. I'll bet it was something to see her in wading – the little cutie pie. You're kind of cute yourself!

We moved back on board this morning, and I must say it is nice to get back to cleanliness, my nice comfortable bunk, and familiarity. By that I mean there are so many things here that you have sent or given me which make it seem as though we are closer together.

I just came down from the movies. We had "Whistling in Dixie" with Red Skelton* – an old picture but very funny. I also had a haircut today. Rather short but not a "beanie". As a matter of fact, I think you would like this one.

Our daughter seems to be rapidly becoming a "glamour girl". All the little boys showing off for her! Guess she really takes after her mom. Not a doubt about it!

Glad to hear the lake looks good to you. I am also happy to hear the bathroom is in. With T'Nookie that will be a big help.

So you changed Margie to Mardy. Well, darling, that is wonderful. Mardy is the only one in the world for me – on birch bark or any other place under the sun.** And you asked me if I mind! I ought to put you across my knee for that. Gosh how I love you. You are without a question the most adorable little chunk of loveliness.

Your last letter only took nine days from way upstate New York which isn't half bad. Gosh but it's wonderful to sort of be in direct communication – I mean you're hearing from me, I'm hearing from you, and we both know the other one is hearing from the other one.

Darling, isn't the lake a wonderful place to make love. The sound of the water, the cool nights, the stars – just you wait! The last time we were there together we were only engaged, but now – oh boy!

Beautiful, I have to rise and shine at 5:30, and as it is now rapidly approaching 11:00 I'm going to say goodnight. Hope your dreams are half as sweet as I know mine will be. I love you with every breath in my body. So much I'll never be able to tell you in a million years just how much.

G'night, angel – I love you.

Donnie

XXXXXXXXX

Whistling in Dixie, starring actor/comedian Red Skelton was made in 1942.[5]

**This letter suggests Mardy may have legally changed her first name. According to the family, however, she always signed her legal documents "Margery."

With the war still smoldering, Donald, tired from training, was losing patience and feeling a loss of control—emotions he had no problem expressing in the following letter. Thoughts of a possible naval career seemed to be evaporating. Despite all of this, Donald could still put into words how he felt about Mardy in the sweetest of ways.

DE Storey, Lieut. (jg) USN
USS Carbonero (SS 337)
c/o F.P.O.
San Francisco, Calif.

Mrs. D.E. Storey
Checkered Rocks
New York
c/o C.E. Storey Jr.

Friday Evening
July 27, 1945
In Port
#15

My Dearest Darling –
Today was such a lucky day. Three letters from you, each one just a bit more wonderful than the other. Darling, I love you so very much that sometimes I think I'm going to bust.

Today was also a long and tiring day. We got underway at 6 am for training and didn't get in until 6:00 tonight.

It sounds as if T'Nook is really having a time for herself at Checkered Rocks. I'll bet she is really a corker. Glad to hear she loves the water so much.

Darling, I want so much to be with you. This certainly is a helpless feeling. Here I am, thousands of miles away with my thoughts, my heart, my desire always with you. I can't wait for this darn war to be over. If the navy intends to try and keep us apart in peacetime – even for short periods of time – I'm going to get out. I'd rather dig ditches and be able to come home to you every night. We wouldn't have money, but we would be happy and that is what counts in life.

Well, perhaps it is time I went sleepy bye. Wish I could put my arms around you and fall asleep with my head in that sweet curve of your neck. Darling, I love you with all my heart and soul. You are my life – my everything. Give T'Nook a big kiss for me.

Yours Forever and Ever,

Donnie

XXXXXX – times a trillion

P.S. This is sort of a dopey letter, but remember I love you, and can't think of anything else.

Still pining for Mardy and wishing he could be at the lake, Donald quickly sat down to write this note just before training exercises. He couldn't seem to believe his daughter was nearing a year old, and it pained him to know four months had passed since his family was together in New London.

DE Storey, Lieut. (jg) USN
USS Carbonero (SS 337)
c/o F.P.O.
San Francisco, Calif.

Mrs. D.E. Storey
Checkered Rocks
New York
c/o C.E. Storey Jr.

Saturday Evening
July 28, 1945
In Port
#16

My Beloved Darling –
We are underway tonight for training, and I don't know how much chance I'll have to write. Will probably be called away before I get very far into this letter.

T'Nook is eleven months old today! Not long now before we'll start thinking of her age in terms of years instead of months. At times, darling, it hardly seems possible she has been a member of our family for this long. Yet again, the last four months have seemed more like years, and it feels like an eternity since we three were together.

Today has been another long one, and it doesn't promise to be much shorter in the hours left to come. First time I've really had a workout in almost two months.

All is well in the Torpedo & Gunnery Department these days. I have really been lucky.

Your experiences with the outboard motor are something. I think you gals need a man around, and I'm just the man for the job. My application is in as of now. All we have to do is convince Uncle Sam that my services are more valuable at the lake than on board the Carbo, and that should be a cinch. Boy, could I defend Checkered Rocks! Wonderful to dream awhile, anyhow.

Darling, I miss you terribly tonight. Every little thing I do recalls a memory – from the moment I open one sleep filled eye until I close my eyes. The period of darkness in between is one in which I do not miss you as we are always together in my dreams. Always close and always happy!

Sweetheart, as I expected I have to run. So for tonight I'll bid a fond au revoir to you and T'Nook. I love you from the bottom of my heart. I always will, dearest.

Yours Forever & Ever,

Donnie

As July was giving way to August, Donald was counting the days to an eventual reunion with his wife and daughter. But first, there was more work to be done aboard the *Carbonero*, and for the country.

Donald sent photos of himself with this note. A small snapshot was found among the letters which may have been one of the two he referred to. Meanwhile, he was still anticipating Mardy's portraits.

DE Storey, Lieut. (jg) USN
USS Carbonero (SS 337)
c/o F.P.O.
San Francisco, Calif.

Mrs. D.E. Storey
Checkered Rocks
New York
c/o C.E. Storey Jr.

Tuesday Evening
July 31, 1945
In Port
#19

My Darling –
Hi angel! How is every little thing tonight? Every day that passes brings us just that much closer to M-D day (Mardy-Donnie day), and every day that passes also finds me loving you more than I did the one preceding – if such a thing is possible.

Today was just a day. I had a long nap in the morning and had the 12–4 watch in the afternoon. Right now it is 5 minutes past midnight, and your sailor boy is sleepy. Have to get up at 5:30 again in the morning.

No mail again today, and we're afraid that it has already been forwarded to our next port of call. What luck! That means a long wait for more news of my sweethearts. However, I can't kick for I have received nearly 50 letters from you since we came in – every one a wonderful epistle from the one I love.

Darling, enclosed are two snaps of a "joker". At least I look as if I have been working hard. They are not very good, but I'm sending them on with a kiss on the lips just for you. By the way, I am certainly anxious to hear how your pictures came out. It took me one heck of a long time to get you to have some taken.

Well, beautiful, until tomorrow I'm going to bid you "sweet dreams, sweetheart". I love you with every bit of me, and I could squeeze you into nothingness tonight. Give T'Nook a big smacker from her Daddy.

I love you, darling –

Donnie

XXXXX

CHAPTER THIRTEEN

The War Ends

On August 4, 1945, The USS *Carbonero* departed the Philippine Islands for her second war patrol in the Gulf of Siam (now the Gulf of Thailand) South China Sea area.[1] With hours to go before he set out, Donald penned the following letter, unaware that it would be less than two weeks before World War II would officially come to an end.

DE Storey, Lieut. (jg) USN
USS Carbonero (SS 337)
c/o F.P.O.
San Francisco, Calif.

Mrs. D.E. Storey
Checkered Rocks
New York
c/o C.E. Storey Jr.

Friday Evening
August 3, 1945
In Port
#22

My Adorable Darling –

Today has been quite a day. Arose early this morning and worked like a Trojan up 'til 2 o'clock, at which time the officers and crew embarked on a ball game and beer party. The officers played the crew, and we beat them two games, 7 to 5 and 3 to 1. After that we all went swimming in a fresh water stream. Boy am I tired now, but it was fun. Remember the ball games in Key West?

I received another super letter tonight. What's this about T'Nook trying to decide who her mother is? I'll spank her little fanny. I think you are just saying that to get a rise out of me.

Hate to see my mail stop coming in and going out, but what must be must be I suppose. Darling, I felt like an awful heel about mother's birthday, and you know how sorry I am if I hurt her. I tried to square things in that letter you know about by now, so hope all is right.

George is on the beach tonight – drunker than a skunk. Not for me, all I want to do is lie down, close my eyes, and dream of you.

Sounds as if T'Nook is getting to be quite a camper. Gosh I wish I could see her looking at the birdies and taking a swim. Bet she is really cute now.

Well, sugar plum, I'm going to say so long until morning. I love you, my darling, more than I ever thought it possible for one person to love another. You are my life, my love, everything I adore.

Sweet dreams, sweetheart.

Your Loving Husband – Now and Forever,

Donnie

XXXXXXXXXXXXXXXX

[No address information available]

August 5, 1945
Sunday Evening
at Sea
#24

My Dearest Darling –

Here I am a hard working man again. Seems good to be at sea again in some ways. Quite a bit cooler and lots healthier. However, the mail situation is no good at all. I certainly enjoyed hearing from you practically every day. Hope it won't be too long before we're hearing from one another again.

I'm standing the 3–6 watches this run. Only a three hour watch for a change. I slept for a short time this morning, and then did a bit of work, wrote some on my notebook, ate lunch, had a nap, and went on watch. Not a very exciting day, and what seems to me to have been a long one.

Darling, every time I think of all the minutes, hours, and days we are missing, I get mad all over. There's no excuse for this damn mess. If only it hurries up and draws to a close.

Well, this is mighty short, but I'm going to hit the hay for a few hours. I love you, darling, with my heart and soul.

Yours Forever,

Donnie

P.S. Dopey letter, don't you think?

On August 6, 1945, the United States dropped an atomic bomb on Hiroshima, Japan. It annihilated the city and immediately killed 70,000 people. 30,000 more would die by the end of the year.[2] Japan was on the precipice of surrender. Donald, however, waited a few days before even mentioning this to Mardy. Instead, he continued to count the months they had been apart. He couldn't help but contemplate when they would have an addition to their family, and painted an ideal picture of how their future would look.

[No address information available]

Monday Evening
August 6, 1945
At Sea

My Darling –

Another day gone – another one closer to the time we will be together again. It has been nearly four months now, and believe me, dearest, these have been long months. Why when we're together four months pass in a wink. I don't understand the inclinations of Father Time.

I just came down from the bridge. A very enjoyable three hours, as it was a gorgeous afternoon – sunny and cool. I spent the better part of the morning working on qualification. I'm bound and determined all three of us will wear dolphins* when this run is over.

What I wouldn't give to be at Checkered Rocks! It must be wonderful up there now. Nice warm days, cool nights, and above all you and T'Nookie. You know what I was thinking about this afternoon? Bet you would never guess. Well I was just wondering – mind you, wondering – not planning – when T'Nookie will have a little brother. What wonderful parties we will have when that time comes! Aren't I an old stinkeroo? I was also daydreaming, once again, about how nice it would be if we were Mr. and Mrs. Instead of Lieut. (jg) and Mrs. Wouldn't it be fun to have a little house around Fairfield,** where you could drive me to the station in the morning and pick me up in the evening? Darling, that sounds good to me, and the navy is going to have to relent on this separation idea or I am going to make a stab at being a "business man". What thinkest thou?

Darling, just out of curiosity, how is our bank account? I know we aren't wealthy, but I'm curious to know how things do stand. I think we are a remarkable couple (ahem!) to do all we've done in such a short space of time and never be in debt.

Is T'Nookie still cutting teeth? Bet she will really be adorable when she smiles with a mouth full of "toofies".

Sweetheart, I'm going to shave before supper, so for today I'll sign off loving you more than ever.

I adore you, beautiful.

Donnie

XXXXX

---

*Donald was referring to the esteemed and hard-earned U.S. Navy submarine warfare insignia featuring two dolphins. The pin indicates the wearer is competent and qualified in submarines.[3]

**A town in southwestern Connecticut.

On August 8, Russia declared war on Japan.[4] Donald wrote this letter the following day, when the United States dropped a second atomic bomb on Japan—this time, Nagasaki was the target. The Japanese entered into surrender negotiations on August 10.[5] Donald was filled with hope. Concurrently, he tried to grasp what the end of the war would mean for his future.

[No address information available]

Thursday Evening
August 9, 1945
at Sea
#27

My Adorable Darling –
First the atomic bomb, and now Russia at war with Japan. Can't last long now. What a wonderful day it will be when all this is over. Doesn't seem possible the end is in sight. Can't quite comprehend what it will be like to settle down and <u>live</u>. I only know that it will be the most wonderful feeling in the world.

How is T'Nook? Wonder what she has been up to lately. She has probably changed so in the past 4 ½ months that I would hardly know her. Does she still sleep with her hands up over her head? If she does that when she sleeps with you, she's batty. I know where my arms would be – right around you, holding on for all I was worth.

Guess what! I am now trying to raise a moustache! Don't believe it will be much of a success as I don't seem to have much of a growth up there. If it turns out, I'll have a picture taken of your "mustachioed" hubby.

Darling, I've lived for 23 years, but the last 19 months and 20 days have been the happiest of all. Even apart from you, I am happy in the knowledge that you are part of me (the better part) – I also have the wonderful future ahead. Years and years of just being with you – I'll never ask for more.

Goodnight, sweetheart. I love you with my heart and soul.
Yours Now and Forever –
Donnie

With Japan's agreement to an unconditional surrender, the end of the war was imminent. At that news, Donald's spirits continued to rise. He was excited and ready to celebrate when he sat down to write this letter, and could hardly contain himself with his declarations of love and the promise that lay ahead.

[No address information available]

Sunday Afternoon
August 12, 1945
at Sea
#29

My Adorable Darling –

I love you, I love you, I love you! Isn't the news of the past 48 hours the most wonderful you have ever heard! Can't quite believe that all we have prayed for, lived for, and waited for is now almost a reality. I can imagine what you are feeling at present. It may be a year before our dreams come true, but it will at least be a year free of worry. It is ironic that with the war's end but a matter of hours I find myself as far from you as I can be and still be on the face of the earth.

I didn't have a chance to write yesterday as we were exceptionally busy, but darling, my thoughts were of you every instant of the day.

What I wouldn't give to be with you now! Boy would we get "stinko".

Just finished a big dinner of turkey, peas, mashed potatoes, and mincemeat pie with chocolate ice cream. Sound good?

My moustache is coming right along – you can even see it now! It's much more comfortable than trying to grow a beard!

Darling, I'm going to try and catch some shuteye as I know I will be up nearly all night. So, for the present, I'll say goodbye – I love you darling, with all my heart.

Yours, Now and Forever –

Donnie

U. S. S. CARBONERO (SS337)

Refer to:
SS337/
Serial #29

℅ Fleet Post Office,
San Francisco, California.

Sunday Afternoon
August 12, 1945
At Sea

My Adorable Darling —

I love you, I love you, I love you! Isn't the news of the past 48 hours the most wonderful you have ever heard! Can't quite believe that all we have prayed for, lived for, and waited for is now almost a reality. I can imagine your feeling at present. It may be a year before our dreams come true, but it will at least be a year free of worry. It is ironic that with the war's end but a matter of hours I find myself as far from you as I can be and still be on the face of the earth.

I didn't have a chance to write

U. S. S. CARBONERO (SS337)

Refer to:
SS337/
Serial

% Fleet Post Office,
San Francisco, California.

yesterday as we were exceptionally busy, but darling, my thoughts were of you and with you every instant of the day.

What I wouldn't give to be with you now! Boy would we get "stinko".

Just finished a big dinner of turkey, peas, mashed potatoes, and mince meat pie with choclate ice cream. Sound good?

My moustache is coming right along - you can even see it now! It's a much more comfortable than trying to grow a beard!

Darling, I'm going to try and catch some shuteye as I know I will be up nearly all night. So, for the present, I'll say goodbye - I love you, darling, with all my heart.

Yours, Now and Forever -

Wonnie

As he stood by for official news of the war's end, Donald vented to Mardy in the following letter. It is imaginable he and the rest of the *Carbonero* crew were on pins and needles waiting to hear that transforming and historic declaration. In the interim, the submarine continued on her short-lived war patrol, taking out some leftovers of the Japanese merchant fleet— schooners, sampans, and junks.[6]

More than likely, Mardy was still at the lake house in upstate New York. Despite the miles between them, they were connected to each other and much of the world in eager anticipation.

[No address information available]

Monday Evening
August 13, 1945
at Sea
#30

Darling –

All day I have been expecting to hear some good news about the war's end – but so far no soap. It will probably take that d– – – red tape outfit in Washington a month to bring this mess to a close. Will be wonderful when there is no more censorship, and I can tell you where I've been and what we have done.

Has T'Nookie learned to swim yet? I'm already getting that old yen for news of my two babies, and we have been at sea just about two weeks! Some guy – I'm a landlubber at heart I'm afraid – I like to at least be where I can hear from my lover baby.

This is my last piece of paper, and as the office is closed I won't be able to steal any more for tonight. So, darling, I'll have to close. I love you, sweetheart – more than you'll ever know. You mean everything in life to me.

Yours always – I love you

Donnie

XXXXXXX

After six long, grueling, and horrific years, World War II finally came to an end on August 14, 1945—August 15 in Japan.[7] August 15 was declared V-J (Victory over Japan) Day.[8]

Donald, although beside himself with the news, was full of uncertainty as to where his service would take him next. He knew it could still be months before he and his family would have their long-awaited reunion.

[No address information available]

Wednesday Afternoon
August 15, 1945
at Sea
#31

My Precious Darling –

Can hardly believe what my heart and head say is true! The war is over! We received the wonderful news this morning in a message which said "Cease all offensive action against the Japanese forces". We are not in any place for celebration – a long long ways from one – but you and I, darling, will have our celebration together. I only hope to high heaven we get ordered to port soon so I can send you a cablegram – otherwise I know you'll worry your adorable head off. If there was only some way I could let you know right now that all is okay.

Naturally everyone is excited. We have no idea what to do next, but we're expecting the worst – having to stay in this part of the world for a good many months till things are all settled down. I'm hoping against hope that such won't be the case, but being a new boat we are probably far down on the list of those returning to the states. In spite of such gloomy thoughts – I've always been a pessimist! – you and I know that it won't be long now before we start living the sort of life we were meant to live – A life of happiness and love *together*.

Bet Checkered Rocks was or is going to be a gay place – probably a few tears too – I know you! Darling, if I could just hold you in my arms for a few hours and tell you all the crazy, happy thoughts that are running around in my noodle.

I'm addressing all your letters to Mt. Vernon as I expect you will be back there by the time I have an opportunity to mail same.

How is T'Nookie today? Tell her that her daddy loves her and is going to come to her or bring her to him at the earliest possible chance. What a wonderful lifetime I have ahead – naval officer or civilian, we don't know which yet – but you, T'Nookie, and lucky Don!

Sweetheart, this has probably been a thoroughly confusing and incoherent letter. Soon as I get my senses collected I'll try and put a little of it on paper. I love you more than I've ever loved life.

Your Adoring Husband Forever,

Donnie

PART THREE

CHAPTER FOURTEEN

Post-War Service

With the cease fire order of August 15, the *Carbonero*'s second war patrol ended and she returned to Subic Bay. On September 22, 1945, the sub arrived at Seattle, Washington for service on the west coast.[1]

According to documentation found with the letters, Mardy left Mt. Vernon, New York, on October 15, 1945, and arrived at Mare Island, California, (the location of the *Carbonero*'s home naval shipyard) on November 5, 1945, to be with Donald. It is not known how long her stay was, but it was at least through Thanksgiving. There were no letters from November to December of that year.

Donald received notification from the Bureau of Naval Personnel in Washington, DC, dated November 23, 1945, that he was granted his qualification in submarines. Documentation found with the letters shows he was awarded his dolphins (the submarine combat insignia) in April of the following year.

By the onset of 1946, the USS *Carbonero* had left the west coast. With the war over, Donald could finally tell Mardy his location. In a partial letter dated January 31, 1946, Donald stated that the submarine was back at Subic Bay and was scheduled to leave on February 10 to go to Shanghai, China, for six weeks to support destroyers. According to the letter, the sub was scheduled to arrive back at the states by July.

No letters survived from February or March. In this April Fool's Day message, Donald was all business. He delivered news of a promotion as the couple planned a reunion and the set up of a temporary home in San Diego, California. The sub's arrival time seems to have moved up.

At this point, Donald stopped numbering his letters.

[No address information available]

Monday Evening
April 1, 1946

My Darling –
I haven't written for the past two days. I just don't know where the time goes. The days seem long, but there don't seem to be enough hours even so! Spent a very quiet weekend.

Dearest, I received a good long letter from you today. I will try to answer all your questions, and I wish I could give you definite information. There has been no change in our tentative orders, but the rumors are still heavy and thick. However, I'm still counting on San Diego in May. Well here come the answers:

1. We will be in San Diego until October or November. After that it will be San Francisco for three months, and after that, well darling, I hope we will be Mr. and Mrs. DE Storey!
2. I think it would be a fine idea to have our household goods shipped out after we are settled.
3. As for setting a definite date for reservations, darling, I'd hold off awhile until I can give you some definite, positive date of arrival. I know that isn't a help in getting reservations, but I really can't say just when we will get to S.D.
4. I don't need to answer this one. We will have a place to live if I have to build it out of orange crates.
5. To the best of my knowledge, I am certain you can ship to Railway Express in San Diego and they will hold it for us.
6. We will claim reimbursement for your travel after we are together. Consequently, I will keep all the papers.

7. I have no idea what our operating schedule will be, but I don't believe it will be Monday to Friday. It will either be daily operations or for a couple of days at a time from all I have heard.

8. And how I love you! I love you so much I could eat you up right this minute.

9. I am counting the days, hours minutes, and seconds until we will be together.

Hope that answers your questions somewhat. I hate to raise your hopes until everything is settled, and consequently, I guess I'm not a very interesting, clarifying, or helpful letter writer. You and T'Nookie just get your things ready and come on out – by train – in a bedroom – and I'll take real good care of you.

Have a surprise for you, sweetheart! An Alnav* came out today making me a Lieut.! That means $70 a month more in our pay check, which will be a big help. All the necessary papers have not been signed yet, but I imagine they will in a day or so.

It is wonderful about having a through train to the west coast. If you and T'Nookie can get a bedroom, it really won't be too bad a trip. I'll be waiting on the platform at the other end with my arms wide open. Oh boy!

I'm all for staying in a Quonset** for a month at least. We'll take our time looking around for a home that we want and that will be within our means. No more horrors like the one we had in New London. How I loved it though – with its falling down kitchen ceiling, its lack of heat in the bedroom, its "immense" closets, and its "moderate" rent.

Oh, angel, as for my white service, don't bother to send them out. Whites are never worn on the west coast. Blue service the year around is the uniform of the day.

Well, darling, I'll be better about writing – I'm not "April foolin" either. I love you with all my heart and soul.

All My Love,
Donnie

---

*An announcement. ALNAV stands for All Navy.[2]

**During World War II, prefabricated metal Quonset huts housed military families.[3]

CHAPTER FIFTEEN

In Command

The plans Donald had for his family in his April Fool's Day letter did not remotely come to fruition. Only a short visit was possible as the Navy had other plans for his service.

According to Donald's records, he remained on the *Carbonero* as Engineering Officer until June 8, 1946. As he noted in a letter dated December 18, 1946, his family was able to be with him in California only from about mid-June until June 23.

Donald was detached from the *Carbonero* on June 25 and reported for air transportation from San Francisco to Honolulu, Hawaii, for his next assignment. In early July he left Honolulu and flew to Tokyo Bay via Guam. He arrived at Tokyo Bay on July 6.

On July 9, 1946, Donald became commanding officer of the *LST-642*, a landing ship tank. Amphibious LSTs were able to unload vehicles, tanks, cargo, and troops directly onto the shore without having to use docks.[1] The vessel was assigned to occupation duty in the Far East during this time.[2]

Just a couple of months later, in another major turn of events, Donald tendered his resignation as a commissioned officer of the United States Navy. He stated in his resignation letter dated September 18, 1946, "I am not best suited for a naval career," and "I can be happier and more successful in civilian life." He requested he be separated from service as soon as possible.

With his resignation being processed, Donald continued on as commanding officer of the *LST-642*. By October, he and his crew were in Japan, which was occupied by the Allied Powers.

There was no more surviving correspondence until October, 1946. As Donald noted in the following letter, Mardy and the baby had returned to the family lake retreat for part of the summer after their short stay in San Diego.

[No address information available]

Wednesday night
October 9, 1946
Yokosuka, Japan

My Precious Darling –
Received three grand letters today. How I wish I could have been at Checkered Rocks with you and T'Nookie! Next summer we'll have to steal a few days up there for sure.

Played basketball tonight and lost again. Expect to start loading vehicles and troops tomorrow, and imagine we will go to sea for the maneuvers about Sunday. Sure will be interested to find out what happens to us when these are all over on October 18th.

Can't imagine what Dad can be making for my Xmas. How about a hint or two?

Darling, I miss you so darn much I'm almost nuts. Everything I see or do in some way or another reminds me of a similar act or sight you and I have witnessed together.

Mighty sleepy at this point, lover baby, as I'll go off to dreamland and you.

Your Adoring,
Donnie

Almost two months had passed since Donald's resignation. By this time, Mardy, the baby, and her parents had moved from Mt. Vernon to Danbury, Connecticut. Donald's many responsibilities as commanding officer only added to the never ending stress of being away from his wife and child, who were now adjusting to a new home that wasn't truly their own.

[No address information available]

Sunday Evening
November 3, 1946
Yokohama, Japan

My Beautiful Wife –
Another Sunday, darling, that has been wasted for us. Won't be too many more of the same after this.

Went to Toyko yesterday afternoon and searched the Ginza – the main shopping district – for something for us, but everything is either outrageously priced or just plain junk. I took my camera along, and someone stole it out of the jeep. Sure glad it wasn't a good camera.

Loading is going slowly, and it looks as if it may be the middle of the week before we can shove off for Nagoya and Kobe. I'd like to get going so I can get back and try and talk these people into sending us to Subic for decommissioning.

Spent most of the day sleeping – got up for lunch but went back again until four this afternoon. Got mixed up with a little too much whiskey at the GHQ* club in Tokyo, and as a result I suffered today – my head was like a balloon!

Are there any little kids nearby for little bit to play with? From her pictures I'd say she still has a devilish gleam in her eye.

The navy done went and lost again! What a year this has been! Wouldn't be surprised to see Notre Dame beat Army next weekend – if they can stop Blanchard!**

Love of my life, it's past midnight, and seeing as how tomorrow is blue Monday, I'd better get my sleep so I can be up and at 'em. Miss you terrifically, darling, and love you more than anything in the world.

Yours Forever,

Donnie

---

*General Headquarters.[3]

**Heisman Trophy winner Felix "Doc" Blanchard was an Army football running back who, from 1944–1946, was instrumental in leading the team to three undefeated seasons in a row.[4]

It was early November and Donald was already thinking about Christmas. Upset he wasn't able to find a suitable present for Mardy, he just as soon would have waited to delay the celebration. But time marched on, and another Christmas would come and go without his family by his side.

DE Storey, Lieut, USN
USS LST 642
c/o FPO, San Francisco, Calif.

Mrs. D.E. Storey
Starrs Plain Rd.
RFD #2
Danbury
Connecticut
c/o Stickles

Monday Evening
November 4, 1946
Yokohama, Japan

My Precious Darling –
This has really been a grey Monday – grey and rainy. Just finished sitting through a movie in the rain. Must have holes in my head. What's more no mail today – all in all not a day of note.

Darling, as I've said before, I don't know what to do about Xmas. Enclosed are two money orders. If you like please take one as a Xmas present, but I'm pretty sure you would rather, I know I would, wait until I get home and have sort of a belated Xmas – just us two. Our own special little Xmas. Darling, I just haven't seen anything you would like and I feel so terrible about it.

That picture of my lover baby, my little lover baby, and T'Nook in the gingham dress is my prized possession. She certainly looks like a doll, and you, angel, look too good to eat. I'm so proud of my family!

We received a letter of commendation for our performance in the amphibious maneuvers, so I guess they were well satisfied with our work.

Darling, I miss you more and more every day, and love you from the tip of your little piggy to the end of one of those grey (my eye!) hairs.

Yours Forever,

Donnie

P.S. Hope you don't think I'm being funny about Xmas

At the end of the month, the *LST-642* was still in service in Japan with an impressive and busy itinerary ahead, and Donald was involved in preparing for the journey. Despite the fact that he would be sacrificing another Thanksgiving at home, he considered himself to be a lucky man.

[No address information available]

Tuesday Evening
November 26, 1946
Yokosuka, Japan

My Precious Darling –

Off on another jaunt through the Japanese empire, starting as of tomorrow. Yokohama, Nagoya, Kobe, Kure, Fukuoka, Nagoya, and Yokohama in that order. Expect we'll be gone until Christmas if not longer.

The Boss called me to the office and told me about the trip. We had a lot of last minute preparations to make, and they consumed the remainder of the day.

No mail today, but we'll probably be in Yokohama for a few days, and will have a chance to receive some more before we finally shove off. Yokohama is just one hour – by jeep or boat – from here.

Wish we were having turkey together this Thursday. I have very much to be thankful for this year.

I love you, darling.

Donnie

Thanksgiving was a day of celebration and rest for the crew of the *LST-642*. Stuffed with food and drink, Donald reminisced about the previous year's Thanksgiving when the couple was able to be together for a short while on the West Coast.

[No address information available]

Thursday Evening
November 28, 1946
Yokohama, Japan

My Beloved Darling –

Happy Thanksgiving Day! Hope you didn't eat as much as your worser half did! We really had quite a dinner. First off yours truly and the pharmacist mixed up a little punch – 190 proof alcohol, grapefruit juice and cherries. All hands had a glass – that's all it takes. The cooks did themselves proud. We had turkey soup, turkey, ham, mashed potatoes, peas, corn, stuffing, pumpkin pie, mince pie, ice cream and all the fixings – olives, nuts, candy etc. All in all, I think everyone enjoyed their dinner.

We came up here yesterday morning and had quite a struggle getting moored due to the current. It rained cats and dogs last night, so we played poker. I lost $10, so now I am a mere $5 ahead on the books. Hope to get away from here before Sunday, but unless they speed up the loading, things don't look too good.

Been wishing I were with you every minute of the day, sweetheart. Remember last Thanksgiving when we had dinner on board the Carbonero in Frisco. Seems like longer than a year to me.

Am enclosing one of our menus. Something else for that scrapbook we are going to have some day. Will be lots of fun fixing it up together.

Just about movie time, so I'll close for today. Tell little bit I hope she liked her turkey. I love you with all my heart, darling.

Yours,

Donnie

It was the end of the month, and the *LST-642* was running behind schedule. Donald hoped to complete the trip through Japan's ports and return to Yokohama by Christmas, but when he wrote this letter, it looked as if his plans might not be realized. To make matters worse, he hadn't received any mail from Mardy, and another holiday away from home was on the horizon. Despite all of this, Donald was buoyed by the fact that Christmas 1946 would be his last Christmas without his family.

[No address information available]

Friday Evening
November 29, 1946
Yokohama, Japan

My Dearest Darling –
Just came in from the movies. We had "Road to Utopia" with Hope and Crosby.* I hadn't seen it before, and consequently, my sides ache from laughing. What a couple of screwballs!

Doesn't look as if we'll get off tomorrow. The army didn't get much done in the way of loading today. This is going to be a mighty long trip – 2456 miles in all. Will really have to move to get back by Christmas. That's my goal, but unless we get on the move soon, I'm afraid we won't have much of a chance.

This ship got mail today, but I wasn't lucky. That usually doesn't happen. Whenever we get mail I nearly always have a letter. Guess this was just one of those days. You've been wonderful about writing, darling, much better than I, I'm afraid.

Enclosed is a snapshot of yours truly – the one in the white hat – on the main deck of my ship. I'm discussing loading 3 LCM's** on deck with my first lieutenant, a naval officer from Kobe, and three Japanese.

Spent most of the day cleaning up some old business and reading official mail. Walked over to the army PX late this afternoon and bought matches, a pack of airmail paper, and a cigarette box (55c) for my desk.

Hate to even listen to the Army-Navy game this weekend. Afraid it will be awful one sided. Would I ever love to see Navy upset the apple cart, but it's not in the cards this year. I wouldn't bet a nickel, cross my heart!

Quite cold tonight – feels almost like winter. Won't be long now before you'll probably be having snow. Darling, I wanted so very much to be home with my two beautiful sweethearts for Christmas, but I guess I shouldn't feel sorry for myself now that I know I'll never have to spend another Christmas away from you. We've batted an even .500 on Christmas – two out of four. Will you ever forget the drive from New London to Mount Vernon two years ago? That was a dilly. Darling, it's going to be so wonderful to make many many more beautiful memories in the years to come.

How's my little pride and joy? Still as fresh as paint – probably fresher! Can't make the days between now and the "day of all days" pass swiftly enough. Goodnight and sweet dreams, sweetheart.

Your Adoring,

Donnie

XXXXXXX

---

*Comedic actors Bob Hope and Bing Crosby partnered to star in seven "road" movies from 1940–1962.[5]

**LCMs or Mechanized Landing Crafts transport vehicles, troops, and cargo from ship to shore and vice versa.[6]

[No address information available]

Saturday Evening
November 30, 1946
Yokohama, Japan

My Dearest Darling –
Here we are almost in December. The months certainly roll by, but far from swift enough at the present time. Wonder where next December will find us. One thing certain, we'll be together.

Just finished three rubbers of bridge. I held good cards for once, and my partner and I won all three rubbers. The movie tonight was "Salty O'Rourke" with Alan Ladd.* All about race horses, so naturally I liked it.

The loading is still not completed, so it looks like Monday at the earliest. My hopes of getting back by Christmas are rapidly failing. Doesn't make too much difference to me personally, as the only Xmas I want I can't have, and we're going to have our own special "tardy Xmas" anyhow. I would like to get the crew back though, so they can receive their mail and take in some of the entertainment which will be provided by the navy. All ports in Japan except Yokosuko are strictly army controlled.

Was up by eight o'clock this morning and helped with inspection of living spaces and machinery compartments – a Saturday morning ritual. No mail again today, darn it.

It's past midnight, and I have to get up early in order to keep poking the army in the ribs to hurry up and finish loading. Hope I get one more letter before we sail! Love you more than anything in the world, darling, and could squeeze you to pieces right now.

Forever and Ever, Your
Donnie

---

*Alan Ladd was a popular movie actor who was known for his roles as a stoic tough guy.[7]

CHAPTER SIXTEEN

Last Christmas Apart

As Christmas approached, Donald became increasingly lonely. With a grueling trip through the Far East ahead of him, Donald sat down and wrote to Mardy at the beginning of December, thinking about the long six months they had been apart.

[No address information available]

Sunday Evening
December 1, 1946
Yokohama, Japan

My Precious Darling –

Still here, but do believe that tomorrow will finally see us underway on the first leg of the trip. The army worked all day loading, and they are practically through.

What did you think about the Army-Navy game? Heard a rebroadcast today, and nearly had heart failure. The navy sure played them off their feet, and I couldn't understand it after the terrible season they have had.

Didn't arise until about 10 o'clock this morning. Sure wished I could rush around at that point helping you get off to church and looking after little bit!

No mail again today. Been over a week now since I've had a letter. The mailman will be making his last trip for quite a while in the morning, and I sure hope he has a present for me when he returns.

What have you and la petite been doing today? For some reason I dislike Sundays more than any other day when we are apart. I love you so much that if something doesn't pop after this trip I'm afraid I'll have to start swimming. We're on our sixth month now – much much too long to be away. Goodnight, angel.

Yours Forever,

Donnie

Little did Donald know when he wrote his December 1 message he would run into complications almost immediately after the outset of his trip. Although a couple of letters in between are missing, we can still piece together the nature of his problems in the following letter. The trouble continued on the day this was written, while the fate of the *LST-642* was yet to be determined.

[No address information available]

Monday Night
December 9, 1946
Yokosuka, Japan

My Beloved –

Surprise – we're back in Yokosuka again. Darling, I haven't written for two or three days, but have been up to my ears. In my last letter I spoke of engine troubles – well things looked so bad that I had to discontinue my trip and come back – arriving here yesterday afternoon.

I have good news. We are going out of commission or being sold to the Koreans on or shortly after 1 January. How do you like that? I'll probably be sitting in here until then trying to get repaired.

Today was a nightmare. A strong wind came up this morning and parted our mooring cables. Spent the rest of today anchoring, weighing anchor and running around the harbor. Finally got tied up to a dock late this afternoon after a momentous struggle against wind and wave.

Received two wonderful letters from you yesterday, sweetheart. You sure finished your Xmas shopping in plenty of time this year. Remember how we rushed around last year trying to find things?*

Darling, I need your loving so very much. Can't wait to see "little bit". Sounds as if she's grown so much in the last five months. Long letter tomorrow – I promise.

I love you,
Donnie

---

*This refers to the time Donald and Mardy were together on the West Coast in 1945.

In his next letter, Donald continued to expound about his ship's troubles. As the days narrowed until he would return to her, he worried whether his little girl would know him upon his return.

[No address information available]

Tuesday Afternoon
December 10, 1946
Yokosuka, Japan

My Dearest Darling –
Last night's letter was very short, and probably a more detailed explanation of how we happen to be back in Yokosuka so soon would make everything a little clearer. As you know we got to Nagoya and unloaded our cargo. Well, one ship's generator which supplies our electricity was already inoperative, and another went out Friday night. That left one – which is not in too good shape, so I called Yokosuka, told them the story and requested permission to return. We left Saturday morning and arrived here Sunday noon. Another LST is finishing our scheduled trip, so guess we will just sit here until January 1 when everything is scheduled to start popping. Don't know yet whether we'll be sold or just plain decommissioned.

Darling, guess I'm really a "short timer" now. Can almost start counting the days! I feel good all over every time I think I'm coming home to my two beautiful gals for good in the very near future. Beautiful, I'm going to love you to pieces. How wonderful it will be to touch you, hear your voice, and look into those devilish eyes. Then, darling, I'll really feel alive again.

When did "little bit" start taking an interest in dolls? She must be growing up a lot faster than I imagined. Hope she'll remember her daddy this time – probably not. From now on she'll know me – of that I'm sure.

Guess that's the dope for today. Darling, I love you with every bit of me and I want you so terrifically.

Now and Forever, Yours Alone
Donnie

In the following message, Donald tried to allay Mardy's fears about their life after the Navy, while not sugar-coating potential struggles they might have. The intense longing he was feeling for her engulfed him. Filled with ardor, he put his heartache into words that had to make her swoon.

DE Storey, Lieut, USN
USS LST 642
c/o FPO, San Francisco, California

Mrs. D.E. Storey
Starrs Plain Rd.
RFD #2
Danbury
Connecticut
c/o Stickles

Wednesday Afternoon
December 11, 1946
Yokosuka, Japan

My Beloved Darling –

Just finished reading four more of your wonderful letters. Can't understand why you don't hear from me more often. I have been writing just about every day, darling – honest injun!

We moved into a dock this morning, and what a time I had with the Japanese pilot and tug boats. Utter confusion! We're in the midst of unloading the remainder of our cargo for transfer to the LST 553.

Darling, in one or two of your letters you have sounded a little worried about our leaving the navy. I want to set you straight once and for all. When we were married it was for love and happiness, and I know I'll be much happier out of the navy. We are going to have a tough time at first, but it's going to be a life together – a life of close intimacy in which we can share all our burdens and worries. I'm sure we'll never regret leaving the navy. Remember, darling, I did this for myself – in a way it's very selfish because you and T'Nookie may both have to get along with less than you would have if we had stayed in the navy.

Sweetheart, I don't believe I've ever missed you more than I have in the past few days. Knowing that the time is so near and yet so far (if you can make any sense out of that!) when we'll be together for once and all just makes the minutes seem like hours. Also the approach of Christmas doesn't help my morale. I wanted to be with you both this Christmas in the worst way possible.

Before I start feeling too blue I'd better lay down my pen and put this in an envelope. Darling, you know how a balloon bursts when it gets just that little too much air inside it – well, that's what troubles me. I'm so filled up with love for you that I'm afraid I'm going to go boom.

I adore you.

Donnie

Although it didn't feel like the holiday season to him, Donald was in high spirits, especially since he received good news about the fate of his vessel. It would remain to be seen, however, if those plans would actually come to fruition.

[No address information available]

Friday Afternoon
December 13, 1946
Yokosuka, Japan

My Beloved Darling –
Just 11 more shopping days until Christmas! You'll never realize it out here – certainly doesn't seem as if Xmas is only 12 days off.

Saw the good news in black and white today. We are to proceed to a disposal port by 1 January, 1947. Where that will be I don't know as yet, but my guess is Subic Bay. Darling, in another three weeks I'll be on the first leg of the trip home – the last trip home.

We've been moving right along the past few days trying to get our two generators back in commission. Weather has been sunny but right cool. Bet I'll really freeze in Connecticut! Maybe not, though, if I can only keep you close enough all the time. That'll keep my temperature sky high. How about it, will you stay real close, all snuggled up?

Expect to get paid in a few days. Sure hope so as I've been broke for weeks, Not that there is anything to spend money on, but I would like to get loose in the souvenir store again with a few dollars. Darling, isn't it going to be a grand feeling to be living in a home with all our things around us and in one spot!

Time for the mailman to leave so I'll close. Hope he brings me a letter in return! I adore you, angel.

Donnie

P.S. Give "little bit" a hug for me!

Donald revealed a variety of emotions in this next letter: excitement about his Christmas presents; relief his little girl was feeling better after a bout with a cold; and the ever-present anticipation of his homecoming. With becoming a civilian on the horizon, he received news of a job opportunity from Mardy.

[No address information available]

Saturday Afternoon
December 14, 1946
Yokosuka, Japan

My Beloved Darling –

How's my sweetheart this afternoon? It has been such a long time, darling.

What did you get me for Xmas? If you don't tell I'll get you when I come home. Am I ever going to get you, anyhow!

Darling, that job your Dad spoke of sounds very lucrative – only thing is I can't be classed as an engineer. I do know <u>something</u> about both mechanical and electrical engineering but just <u>something</u>. However, it sounds mighty interesting at present.

Sorry to hear "little bit" had a cold. Must have missed a letter or two as in this one you said her cold was better.

We were paid today, but I only received a pittance – $40 – as we were docked for our mess bills for Sept., Oct., and Nov. – what a terrible situation!

The work is coming along smoothly, and we will be already to go by Xmas. Darling, the way I figure I should be home a civilian around March first, unless there is a holdup someplace along the way.

Time for supper, so I'll close for today. I love you with all my heart.

Donnie

[No address information available]

Monday Evening
December 16, 1946
Yokosuka, Japan

My Adorable Darling –

One more "blue" Monday just about behind us. Not too many more of the same to come now. No day will ever be blue when I can start it by waking up beside you and stealing a kiss.

Today I managed to remain fairly busy all day. Walked down to the souvenir shop this afternoon to purchase a blue cap cover – that being the uniform since yesterday. There was the most gorgeous string of pearls on display for only $220! How I wish I had that much. They would look so beautiful on you, darling.

No mail for the past two days. Tomorrow should see some improvement – I hope. Darling, I sure am lonely. I was just thinking what a feeling it is going to be to be with you and T'Nookie and know for certain that we won't ever be separated by long periods of time. Afraid it will be like a dream for a while. No shadows to darken our days, angel. That will be a novelty. Always before, separation has hovered just over the horizon.

I'll love you forever,

Donnie

With Christmas less than a week away, Donald was caught up in sending gifts to his family. Thoughts of coming home consumed him. Deprived of any interaction with his child for so long, he felt like a stranger to her. All he wanted to do was spend some time with his family to readjust and build the bonds the war had postponed.

DE Storey, Lieut, USN
USS LST 642
c/o FPO, San Francisco, Calif.

Mrs. D.E. Storey
Starrs Plain Rd.
RFD #2
Danbury, Connecticut
c/o Stickles

Wednesday Evening
December 18, 1946
Yokosuka, Japan

My Beloved Darling –
Sent you a Xmas cablegram today and I do hope it arrives in time. Also, darling, remember that box I was to have mailed about six weeks ago? Well I finally sent it off today, by air mail, so it should reach you in two or three weeks. I really tried to send it off the last time, but the post office said it was not packed strong enough. Cost me $11 to send the package and I am now almost broke again. More fun! Had to transfer my engineer to the LST 1010 because they are short on officers. That leaves me with three – probably end up like I started – the lone wolf.

Darling, all I can think about is coming home. I day dream, night dream, build air castles, plan, reminisce, and just plain think about us – all three of us. Let's just take two weeks to catch up on our lives and our love before we settle down to the actualities of life. Just two weeks in which you, snookie, and I can get acquainted as a family. Perhaps that sounds strange, but I don't feel that I really know "little bit". After all I have seen so little of her since she has started talking.

In five days, six long (and I do mean long!) months will have passed since we were together. Has really been almost two years since the three of us were really together. Didn't even get your trunk fully unpacked in San Diego.

Still no definite departure date yet, but the wheels are beginning to turn. I rather expect we'll leave prior to the first of the year. I can't wait to get started. Every mile I travel will mean a mile closer to you, darling, and that's what I'm after for the rest of my life – to be close to you. Come hell or high water that is where I'll always be – with you. Sweetheart, I love you with such an overwhelming passion and devotion that it often scares me. I just want to spend the rest of my life proving the last sentence – how very much I do adore you.

Your own,

Donnie

[Western Union Telegram]

YOKOSUKA 1946 DEC 18 338P
MRS. D E STORY
STARRS PLAIN RD RFD 2 DANBURY CONN
MERRY XMAS DARLING MY THOUGHTS AND LOVE ARE WITH
YOU ALL
CATCH LITTLE BIT UNDER THE MISTLETOE FOR ME ALL MY
LOVE DON

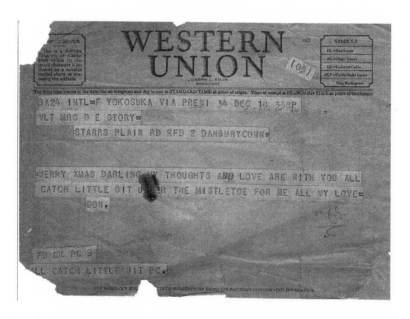

In the early morning hours of December 21, 1946, a massive undersea earthquake and tsunami struck southern Japan, killing more than a thousand people and causing mass destruction.[1] If Donald knew about the severity of this disaster, he downplayed it for Mardy's sake in this letter.

A day earlier, Donald made sure the *LST-642* was decorated for the holiday, though his efforts were half-hearted. Back home, Mardy got into a bit of trouble with the car and as a result, received a scolding from her husband. And in the cutest of developments, their daughter claimed another piece of her daddy's heart.

DE Storey, Lieut, USN
USS LST 642
c/o FPO, San Francisco, Calif.

Mrs. D.E. Storey
Starrs Plain Rd.
RFD #2
Danbury, Connecticut
c/o Stickles

Saturday Evening
December 21, 1946
Yokosuka, Japan

My Precious Darling –
I think our Christmas cards are extremely nice, darling. Received two letters from you this morning, one of which was written on one of our Xmas cards.

Yesterday afternoon, Smitty (my first lieutenant), and myself went up in the hills and cut two Xmas trees for the ship. I managed to buy some decorations, so at least we will have a Xmas tree. We also made a big star with lights all around the edge that we have placed on top of the mast. In spite of everything, I can't seem to feel much of a Xmas spirit.

There was a tidal wave in southern Japan this morning, but it did not have any effect on us. Guess a small earthquake started it.

In a letter from mother I received this morning she spoke of Snookie saying "let's play As Time Goes By. That's mommie's and daddy's song". That knocks me for a loop. The little "cutie pie". What a daughter we have, sweetheart!

Glad your affair with the state troopers didn't result in trouble. Driving without your license! I'm sure going to have to hurry home and take care of you – in more ways than one.

How's the dawg? You haven't mentioned him lately, so I guess he hasn't been causing any trouble.

Time for supper, so I'll sign off for today. I love you with all my heart, adorable one.

Your Own,

Donnie

DE Storey, Lieut, USN
USS LST 642
c/o FPO, San Francisco, Calif.

Mrs. D.E. Storey
Starrs Plain Rd.
RFD #2
Danbury, Connecticut
c/o Stickles

Monday Evening
December 23, 1946
Yokosuka, Japan

My Precious Sweetheart –
Six long months – darling, it has been such a long time. Seems to me as if I have been away for six years.

We spent most of the day yesterday making lights, painting lights, and decorating our wardroom tree. It really looks very nice. Still can't grab hold of the Xmas spirit, however. Darling, I am going to miss you so much tomorrow and Xmas day. What I wouldn't give to be able to go to midnight mass with you tomorrow night!

Wish I could express my emotions and my thoughts at this point. If only I could make my love as strong on paper as it is in my heart. I used to think I could write, angel, but I can't find words that will express how deeply I love you. I am the luckiest man alive.

Goodnight, my love.
Donnie

As his feelings of isolation from his family reached new heights, Donald sat down on Christmas Eve to write this poignant letter. In an encapsulation of their journey together, Donald described how their awkward beginning grew into a love so strong it simply could not die. The conclusion of this letter is sheer poetry.

DE Storey, Lieut, USN
USS LST 642
c/o FPO, San Francisco, Calif.

Mrs. D.E. Storey
Starrs Plain Rd.
RFD #2
Danbury, Connecticut
c/o Stickles

Christmas Eve, 1946

My Beloved –

Can't help but feel a little blue today, in spite of what is called "the holiday season". We have so many memories wrapped up in the last four Christmas days, darling. Four years ago tonight you took Buggy for what was to become one of the most beautiful walks in the world. I was certainly a heel that night, but though my methods were crude the results were beautiful. Darling, I am so completely in love with you that I feel somehow that we were really made for one another.

No snow here for Xmas. Hope you have a snowfall tonight. Hope you can remember every detail of Snookie's Christmas – I'm so anxious to hear all about her reactions.

Darling, it will certainly be a very happy Christmas a year from now – our first in our own home. I know you are going to have a wonderful Christmas this year too – all of you. All mother and dad have talked about is spending Christmas with you and "little bit". It will be such a happy day for them.

All my love, my thoughts, my dreams, and my hopes are with you tonight, dearest. Could I but hop on a star and glide to where you are. If only for a moment – a moment of beauty and love that would cause all the separating miles and hours to pale and fade away. No stars for rent, sweetheart, but I'll be around in my own special dream boat sometime between now and the dawn.

A very Merry Christmas, darling, to you and our Snookie.

I adore you,

Donnie

Christmas Eve, 1946

My Beloved –

All my love, my thoughts, my dreams, and my hopes are with you tonight, dearest. Could I but hop on a star and glide to where you are. If only for a moment – a moment of beauty and love that would cause all the separating miles and hours to pale and fade away. No stars for rent, sweetheart, but I'll be around in my own special dream boat sometime between now and the dawn.

PART FOUR

CHAPTER SEVENTEEN

As the new year began, Donald was still serving in Japan as commanding officer of the *LST-642*. The original plans for the vessel to proceed to a disposal port by January 1 did not materialize, and neither did his hope to be home by the first of March. Donald's letters to Mardy, who was still living with her parents in Connecticut, continued to express his aching for the day he would finally return home.

Mardy's frustration with the continual delays had to echo Donald's. Most likely, she was losing patience as well. It was inevitable that her continually dashed hopes would have an effect on her psyche.

Only two of Donald's letters survived from January, 1947. In the following note, he referred to the family dog Mr. Chips, who had an unfortunate accident. Things were still going slowly with loading operations and Donald's spirits were as dreary as the weather.

[No address information available]

Sunday afternoon
January 26, 1947
Okinawa

My Dearest Darling –

So sorry to hear about Mr. Chips being hit by a car. Hope he recovers speedily. Was "little bit" very upset over his accident?

Thus far, little has been accomplished towards getting the good LST 642 loaded. However, we did recover our stern anchor yesterday which is quite a load off my mind. I have had every assurance that we will be loaded and sent on our merry way as quickly as possible, but it looks like a good two week layover unless the loading goes much better than it has so far.

Not a very nice day. It has been raining and cloudy all day. I have spent the better part just puttering. Now have all four of my lighters in first class operating condition.

It has been quite some time now since you have sent any snapshots. How about some of both my sweethearts. The best I usually get of you is a rear view. Not that I object as I have always been in love with your rear (view). Remember how furious that used to make you?

It is now late in the evening. The weather is just as crummy, and, having holes in my head, I went out and sat through the movie in the rain.

Darling, I guess that's all the news and views for tonight. I'm just counting the days until we will be together. At times this all feels like a bad dream, and it's going to be delightful to wake up and find you in my arms.

Goodnight, love of my life.

I adore you,

Donnie

Two days later, Donald's mood was lifted by the arrival of some letters, and he was amused to learn that his little girl had developed quite a personality. Things on board remained the same, as he and his crew tried to stay on track with their assignment. At the end of his message, he imagined what it would be like to hold Mardy in his arms again.

[No address information available]

Tuesday Evening
January 28, 1947
Okinawa

My Precious Darling –
Today was quite a lucky day as I received three letters from my beautiful wife. They were not as late as two letters I received at the end of last week, but they were wonderful anyhow.

This loading proposition is certainly a slow one, but we should be finished before a week is up unless there are some unforeseen holdups ahead.

So our "little bit' has a temper! Wonder who she inherited that from. Rather imagine she acquired some from both her mother and her father.

Darling, there are times when I torture myself with visions of gathering you into my arms and feeling us become as one. I will ask for nothing more than to be able to do that every day for the rest of our lives.

Yours Forever,
Donnie

February started with the *LST-642* in Okinawa engaged in the slow process of cargo loading. To combat the drudgery, the crew took part in some extra-curricular activities. Donald was wondering about Mr. Chips, and enclosed a photo of the crew's dogs with the following letter, but it did not survive. He was still concerned he wouldn't recognize his daughter when he finally saw her, and mused again about having another child. Mardy's 24th birthday was coming up, and he attempted to make some long distance celebratory arrangements for her.

[No address information available]

Sunday Evening
February 2, 1947
Okinawa

My Precious Darling –
I'm becoming downhearted about the rate at which the loading is proceeding. The one bolster to my morale is that there is an end to this foolishness – the day when I take you in my arms never to relinquish you 'til "death do us part."

Last night we had a smoker consisting of seven boxing bouts with the LST 865. We won four of the fights, and consequently won the smoker. A good time was had by all. This afternoon we had a ball game among ourselves and my team won 16–15 – sounds more like football. Aside from the athletic side, your husband has been leading a Spartan like existence – early to bed and early to rise.

Darling, I hope the plans I tried to formulate for your birthday worked out. Don't believe I've ever been away from you on so many important days as I have this time.

How's Mr. Chips? Haven't had any letters later than the one in which you were so worried about him because he wouldn't eat.

Gosh, I'll bet I won't even know our daughter. From all your letters, I'm beginning to realize that we no longer have a baby – 'tis a little girl our "little bit" has become.

In about another year, we will have to talk about a brother for our Snooker. How about it?

Enclosed is a snapshot of our two pups – both of them look scared to pieces. They are a great deal larger than when the picture was taken.

I love you so much, darling, that sometimes I feel as if my heart will pop from too much love. I've missed you a lot in the past, but never as much as I do now. You will look so wonderful to me.

Yours Forever,

Donnie

Donald composed this letter the afternoon of Mardy's birthday. While despondent he couldn't be with her, he tried to make light of the situation. However, by the end of his message he was all too willing to tell her how he really felt.

[No address information available]

Tuesday afternoon
February 4, 1947
Okinawa

Happy Birthday darling –
Wish I could be with you today to celebrate a very lucky day for me. I certainly was a happy little fellow of eleven months when I heard that my beautiful bride to be had arrived. Hardly seems as if twenty four years have gone by since then. Hope you had a grand time on your birthday. I'm going to go up to the local club this evening and have one drink for you – hardly a fit way to celebrate, but we'll make up for all these missed celebrations next year and in all the years to come.

No good news at this end of the line, darling. Time is hanging very heavily on my hands, and from all appearances it will be at least another week before we're ready to start on our merry way once again. Every time it rains, they don't load, and today it is pouring – fine thing!

Darling, after I realized I couldn't be with you on Christmas, this was the next goal, but here we are as far apart as ever. I need you so much, darling. I married you because I love you and want to be with you always, but in the past three years and three and a half months being with you where I can hear you, see you, touch you, and love you has been a very small percentage of the time we've had to carry on our lives via pen and paper. I'm certain I will feel I'm dreaming for the first year we are together. To wake up every morning and see you beside me – real close up – honest, darlin, it's all I'll ever ask for.

Well, birthday child, this has been rather an incoherent letter but I'm not apologizing. All my love and kisses are always yours, sweetheart.

Your Own,
Donnie

Donald shared more news of the progress with cargo loading in this letter, and we learn the fate of Mr. Chips the dog. The couple's song, which connected them across the miles and over the years, sparked sadness in Donald after he heard it played on the radio. Mardy was visiting Donald's aunt and uncle in New York when he wrote this message.

DE Storey, Lieut, USN
USS LST 642
c/o FPO, San Francisco, Calif.

Mrs. D.E. Storey
Wolfs Lane
Pelham
New York
c/o Lawler

Sunday Evening
February 9, 1947
Okinawa

My Dearest Darling –

Haven't written for a couple of days, and even so there is not much news. We are fairly well loaded, and are supposed to move to a pier to complete same, but so far haven't been able to retract from the beach. Too much weight on the bow. Have two tugs coming tomorrow to assist.

No mail for the past few days. Hope you are continuing to write as often as possible for I live for your letters.

Night before last a mosquito really gave me the business. When I woke up yesterday morning I couldn't even recognize myself. My right eye was swollen so I could hardly open it, and my lip was at least four times its normal size. Thought for a minute I had been fighting in my sleep, but then the buggar flew by and I made short work of him. The swelling disappeared in a few hours, but was I ever a sight!

Our two pups are certainly growing by leaps and bounds. Blackie looks as if he's going to be a grand looking dog. Thinking seriously of trying to bring him home for Snookie to replace Mr. Chips. Afraid we'd have a time house breaking him after he's been living aboard a ship!

The Cabezon – B.B. S.'s old sub is due in here shortly. Wonder if he's still on board. Sure would like to see both he and Chipmunk again. We had lots of fun with them in New London, even at the Penn game where my "child bride" couldn't get a drink served. I'll never forgive myself, for not punching that bar keep in the nose right then and there.

Darling, I heard "As Time Goes By" this afternoon with Ginny Simms* singing. Certainly made me feel blue.

Lover baby, It's movie time and for once I haven't seen the picture – "Destry Rides Again".** Will close for now and will be better about writing this week. Give my daughter a hug and kiss for her daddy. I've got millions of them stored up for you sweetheart.

I love you,
Donnie
XXXXXXX
OOOOO

---

*Ginny Simms was a band singer and actress who, during the '40's, had her own national radio program.[1]

**A 1939 movie starring James Stewart and Marlene Dietrich.[2]

By the end of the month, the *LST-642* had arrived in Saipan, a Mariana Island in the western Pacific. The island was captured by the Allies in 1944 and by 1947 it had become a major U.S. air base.[3] Donald was happy things were picking up with the loading process and tried to enjoy some of the nightlife and activities the island offered.

DE Storey, Lieut, USN
USS LST 642
c/o FPO, San Francisco, Calif.

Mrs. D.E. Storey
Starrs Plain Rd., RFD #2
Danbury, Connecticut
c/o Stickles

Monday
February 24, 1947
Saipan

My Precious Darling –
Finally arrived here yesterday morning, for what I hope will be a short stay. First impressions gathered lead me to believe that we will be here only for a short time. They really turned to unloading us this morning. We have to load some scrap for the U.S. I'm not sure whether we will go to San Diego or not – possibly San Francisco.

There was no mail waiting for us. Hope we at least get a few letters before leaving. Won't be much longer before letters will no longer be a necessity.

Ran into a classmate of mine who used to be in submarines and is now skipper of an LSM.* According to him practically the entire class is or has resigned. He and I went up to the local club last night for a few drinks. It is a very pretty club, situated way up on a hill overlooking the ocean.

It's grand to have some warm sunny weather. Fairly hot – 92 degrees yesterday. You people are probably freezing at this point, so I won't rub it in!

There is a golf course, of all things, on the island, and I am contemplating trying my luck tomorrow. Probably I will be awful.

The unloading crew did more in one day than Okinawa did in four. Looks like we'll get out of here in short order.

Had "Notorious"** for a movie tonight. Not much of a story, but Ingrid Bergman is always good.

Certainly miss you an awful lot, darling. Every day we are apart seems such a waste of time.

I love you,
Donnie

---

*An LSM, or Landing Ship, Medium, was a smaller version of the LST.[4]
**A 1946 Alfred Hitchcock movie, nominated for two Academy Awards.[5]

CHAPTER EIGHTEEN

The Long Journey Home

It had been six months since Donald's official resignation from the Navy, but during the first half of March he remained in Saipan in command of the *LST-642*, following the orders of his superiors. Finally, in the middle of the month, the ship started to make her way back to the states, but not without some discouraging setbacks.

[No address information available]

Sunday
March 2, 1947
Saipan

Mardy Darling –

Still no mail for us, and it's beginning to look as though we're going to have to wait a long while before we do receive any. I sure could use a couple of letters.

We are just half way unloaded, so about another week should find us ready to sail. Sounds as though we will go to Frisco. They haven't much cargo for us, but I think we will carry a few passengers.

Friday I took Blackie to a local veterinarian and had him shot for rabies. Got his clearance to enter the states, so now he can be a citizen. He's an awful cute puppy, but it looks as if he's going to be quite a large dog. His paws are big, and his tail is long.

We were paid Friday, and I put $300 away in my safe. I think we're going to have enough to get us settled, darling, what with the mustering out money and all.

According to the local news paper, you've been up to your neck in blizzards and sub freezing temperatures this last week. Bet you're really snowed in down on the "farm".

Darling, I am becoming very impatient to say goodbye to the navy and kiss you and T'Nookie hello. I'm so terribly in love with you, darling, that the world holds no attraction for me when we are apart. I'd trade the most precious gem there is for one kiss from you. Give "little bit" a hug for her daddy.

I adore you,

Donnie

XXXXXXXXXX

It appeared as if the world was conspiring against Donald in his quest to arrive back to the states in a timely fashion. When he wrote this letter, another monkey wrench had been thrown into the works. With circumstances beyond his control, Donald had reached the height of exasperation.

DE Storey, Lieut, USN
USS LST 642
c/o FPO, San Francisco, Calif.

Mrs. D.E. Storey
Starrs Plain Rd., RFD #2
Danbury
Connecticut
c/o Stickles

Thursday Evening
March 13, 1947
Saipan

My Precious Darling –

I had a premonition that I could not return to the states without some way or another being ordered to go via Pearl Harbor. Well, it happened this morning. We received a message from Commander Service Force, Pacific Fleet, directing us to tow a small oiler from here to Pearl Harbor. Such order will involve nothing but headaches for me and extra time apart for us as the tow will slow us down considerably. At this stage, I'm about ready to beat my noggin against the nearest bulkhead. The one consolation is that we received the message before we were about three days at sea, in which case we would have had to backtrack. Really keeping my fingers crossed for good weather, particularly so with a ship in tow.

Darling, I'm trying my darndest to get home, but everything seems to be working against me. Gosh knows we're having a tough enough time getting back ourselves without adding the woes of a towed vessel. I am nearly ready to lose my sense of humor.

I spent all morning haggling about the method to be used in towing this lame duck, and I sure hope my ideas are sound. Still plan to leave here Saturday.

Played baseball this afternoon and lost 5–3. Are you sure this isn't Friday the 13th. Oh well, darling, when we're old and gray we can look back on all this and laugh I suppose, but I sure am ready to start putting this era behind us. The future is so much more attractive than the present.

Hope to have two or three more letters from you tomorrow. Will be the last chance for about three weeks. You have been wonderful about writing lately, angel.

Have a full day ahead tomorrow shifting berth, hooking up the tow, etc., and as I'm a mite weary I think it's about time I hit the hay.

I love you, darling, and someday soon we'll be together as one again so that I can tell you just how very much you mean to me.

Goodnight darling,

Donnie

Donald wrote this message a day before his 25th birthday, after having received a card and letters from Mardy. Soon he and his crew would be underway, slowly inching toward Pearl Harbor. In anticipation of their reunion, Mardy was getting ready by setting up furnishings for their future home.

[No address information available]

Friday Evening
March 14, 1947
Saipan

My Dearest Darling –
Your birthday card arrived today – very good timing, angel, and thank you ever so much. Also received two more grand letters from you.

We have just about finished loading, and as soon as we get this towing lash up straightened out we'll be on our way. Will most likely take about three weeks to Pearl Harbor with this darn ship in tow.

Darling, I hope you were able to buy the end tables. Sounds like a marvelous buy if they were what you wanted. Aren't we going to have fun furnishing our own place. Perhaps we'll have to do it in degrees, but everything we have will be ours – something we bought together.

Have to rise early again tomorrow, so I'd better get to sleep. I love you, my darling, and think only of the day when I take you in my arms never to let you escape from them again.

Yours Forever,
Donnie

The *LST-642* was finally on her way to Pearl Harbor with the tow when Donald wrote this St. Patrick's Day message. He knew all too well it would be a long, slow, and arduous trip. He described his birthday celebration, and while it was tempered because of his separation from Mardy, he had an enjoyable time.

[No address information available]

Monday Evening
March 17, 1947
at Sea

Mardy darling –
Underway once again, and this time I will be coming 3200 miles closer to you. Had quite a struggle hooking up our tow and clearing the harbor, but with the aid of a tug and lady luck all was accomplished with no mishaps. Now, as long as we have decent weather, all should go well until we reach Pearl Harbor in about three weeks. With this darn tow we only average around six or seven knots per hour.

Darling, my birthday was as much of a success as any day away from you can be. The cooks baked me a huge birthday cake, one of my Filipino boys presented me with four cartons of cigarettes and a card I can't wait to show you, and I managed to get mellow at the club – all in all not a bad day.

It's a coincidence, darling, but at this exact date last year I was almost in the same spot going the same way. One thing certain, never again will this day find me away from you.

Yours Forever,
Donnie

Donald's patience was being tested in endless ways, from the burden of his tow to the constant uncertainty about when his journey, and his service, would end. Riding an emotional rollercoaster as well as the waves, all Donald could think about was Mardy and going home.

[No address information available]

Tuesday Evening
March 18, 1947
at Sea

Hi darling –

We are still kicking along at a slow rate of speed. The tow is still following meekly astern, thank goodness!

Darling, you'll never know what a torture these past few months have been. I suppose it has been a good lesson in the value of patience, but there have been times when I've seen red at all the delays which have occurred. Gosh knows I'm more than willing to do all I can for the navy as long as they need me, but once in awhile it seems as if they are needing my services just a trifle over long. Oh well, can't be too much longer. Every mile that goes astern is shortening the time and distance until we will be together.

I have so much to tell you, so much to ask you, and so many plans to discuss with you. Better store up on sleep, darling, 'cause between love making, fun making, and talk making I'm not going to give you any chance for shuteye.

Darling, I'll write you every day to let you know how we're progressing. Wish this darn tub was jet propelled or sompin.

I love you,
Donnie

[No address information available]

Friday Evening
March 21, 1947
at Sea

My Dearest Darling –

This letter may prove rather difficult to read in view of the fact we're bouncing all over the ocean tonight. Weather is not too bad, but it is windy and a moderate sea is running. That's all it takes to make a cork of this hunk of iron.

The days are passing very slowly, and imagine they will pass slower yet as we draw nearer to Pearl Harbor. I'm up before sunrise every morning in order to take star sights and find out just where we is. Haven't been able to sleep much during the day, as the tow makes me somewhat nervous and I can't sleep unless I am good and tired. Sure hope the d– – – thing stays hooked on until we reach Pearl. It would be one devil of a job trying to recover it in weather like this.

Well, better make this short as it is difficult to write, and I imagine will be even harder to read. I love you very much, beautiful.

Yours Forever,

Donnie

Donald's hopes of being reunited with his family by Easter were quickly dashed. Threatening world events lurked on the horizon, and he was right to be concerned about them. Still, thoughts of his family reunion kept him going from day to day.

[No address information available]

Tuesday Afternoon
March 25, 1947
at Sea

My Beloved Darling –

Still poking along at about six knots. Doesn't seem as if we are getting any-place, but I suppose we'll arrive someday. The good weather is still with us, but what sea and wind there is is from dead ahead and helps hold down our speed. We haven't had a bit of trouble with the tow so far, and am I ever thankful. It looks now as if we will arrive in Pearl around Easter Sunday. Gosh, darling, I was certain we'd be together by Easter at least!

Shouldn't be long now before nice weather comes to Connecticut. From the picture your mother sent, I should imagine that it is a lovely spot in the spring.

The news is certainly frightening! Wish these d– – – politicians would stop talking war with Russia.* If there's another war, all the big talkers should be in the first wave to hit the beach. Perhaps then peace would be their aim instead of war mongering.

Darling, I am certainly looking forward to the day we are going to start living together like normal people for the rest of our lives. I have missed you so much these past nine months that I know I'll never be able to let you out of my sight again. I dream night and day of just how soft and lovely you are and how very much I want to feel you in my arms again. I love you, darling, so very much.

Your Own,

Donnie

P.S. Give little bit a big kiss for me.

---

*After the war ended, any alliances between the United States and Russia (Soviet Union) dissolved quickly. Under Joseph Stalin, Russia occupied Eastern Europe in a power move. In 1947, with Greece and Turkey earmarked to be next, President Truman asked Congress for aid to help the U.S. and Britain prevent the Soviets from overthrowing the two countries.[1] In the Communists' eyes, this action cemented the Cold War.[2]

As March drew to a close, Donald was still plagued with problems aboard the *LST-642*. Consequently, she continued to move at a snail's pace. Duty called, and any hopes of brushing past Pearl Harbor dissolved as the ship's needs took precedence over Donald's.

[No address information available]

Monday afternoon
March 31, 1947
at Sea

My Dearest Darling –

I have been somewhat of a "stinker" about writing this past week. We have been moving along very slowly and have had more than our quota of engine trouble. Will take us another eight to ten days to reach Pearl at the present rate. The weather has been fair, but not calm enough for easy towing. However, our tow hasn't tried to leave us yet.

I was planning to try and keep right on going past Pearl as soon as we transferred our tow, but now it looks as if we had better stop for a few days and make a few repairs. Someday, angel, I'll be home to you. Won't be surprised if a whole year will have been taken from our lives though. One thing sure, beautiful, this past nine months has convinced me once and for all that I could never have been happy in the navy. I never want to leave you for any length of time again as long as we both shall live. I mean that with all my heart.

If we are in Pearl Harbor long enough, I'm going to call you, but I'll telegraph at any rate. It takes 24 to 48 hours to place a call.

Darling, I feel rotten that you won't have flowers from me Easter morning. I was hoping to be in Frisco just about then and surprise you with a call.

Darling, I'll try and write every day until we reach port. I miss you terribly, and love you to pieces. Give my "big girl" a kiss and a squeeze. I have plenty of both saved up for you.

Yours Forever,
Donnie

CHAPTER NINETEEN

Return to Pearl Harbor

Early April found Donald in great anticipation of reaching Pearl Harbor, and starved for information from Mardy. A mariner's lucky charm was in the air, but the ship, the sea, and the U.S. Navy would continue to determine when this officer could finally call himself a civilian.

[No address information available]

Thursday Evening
April 3, 1947
at Sea

My Darling –
Another week should find us in Pearl Harbor. For the past twenty four hours we've been running along very smoothly, and I have my fingers crossed in the hope of not having more engine trouble. This has certainly been one long, slow trip.

We must have about twenty albatross following us. To a sailor they signify good fortune, but ours have not been too excellent. In spite of all the engine trouble, losing the tow would have caused a greater waste of time and energy, so perhaps we have had good luck after all.

If I don't become a civilian soon, I'm going to be walking around in virtual tatters. Nearly all my clothes are showing signs of great wear now

– plenty of frayed cuffs and collars. It is going to be such fun outfitting in civilian style. Wonder how you'll like me in "civvies"?

Darling, I detest going so long without hearing from you. I try to visualize what you are doing and thinking every minute of the day, but with such a difference in time I know I seldom have you at the right place, doing the right thing, at the right time.

I love you so very much, dearest, and miss both my best girls every second of the day.

Yours Forever,

Donnie

Easter arrived on April 6, and Donald began this love note with a sweet takeoff on the song "Easter Parade" written by Irving Berlin, followed by a warning to Mardy that once he returned home, she'd never be free of him. Finally, there was a glimmer of light at the end of the tunnel.

[No address information available]

Easter Sunday, 1947
at Sea

My Beloved –
"In your Easter bonnet
　With all the ribbons on it
　I know you were the most beautiful lady
　In the Easter parade"
Hi angel – does you love me as good as I love you? Not half as much I'm willing to wage!

Still bumping along, but all should be quiet come Thursday. Not for longer than is absolutely necessary if I have my way. Just take aboard fuel and water and then start towards the Golden Gate. This has really been a long trip. Twenty two days already and still no land in sight! What a navigator! I'm ready to sell this hunk of iron to the Gillette company any time now. It would probably make a few million extra fine razor blades.

Darling, it is really going to be a treat to change the age old expression "Long time no see" to "Long time no sea." I will never even cross the lake in a rowboat unless you are sitting on the seat beside me! I wonder if you realize what a problem you are going to have on your hands. I'm warning you right now that I don't intend to let you out of my arms for the first month or out of my reach for the first year or out of my sight for life. I'll let the rest of the people watch the world go by and just sit and watch you. It is so wonderful to love the way I love you. All else in life pales in insignificance when I think about you and how wonderful you are. Gosh, ain't life grand – at least it is going to be!

Supper time, darling, if you were here I'd give up eating for a month and just make love. Every night will be party night, angel.   .

Yours Forever and Ever,

Donnie

P.S. I love the "little one' awful good too.

[Western Union Telegram]

HONOLULU
MRS. D E STOREY STARRS PLAIN RD RFD NUMBER 2 DANBURY, CONN
1947 APR 12 AM 10 56
DARLING FINALLY ARRIVE THIS AFTERNOON WHAT A TRIP I LOVE YOU SO VERY MUCH
DON

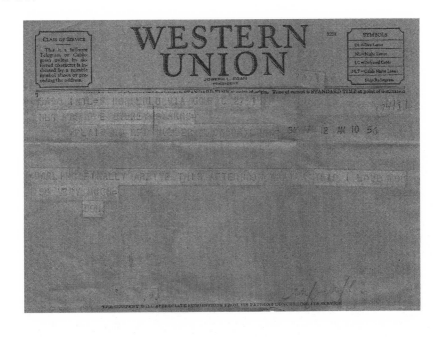

At long last, the *LST-642* had arrived at Pearl Harbor. Donald wrote this letter the day after wiring Mardy the news. His relief to be in port was short-lived, however. There was another problem with the ship and new orders from his superiors. On top of that, he couldn't even place a call to his wife because of a telephone strike. At this point, Donald was ready to throw in the towel.

[No address information available]

Sunday
April 13, 1947
Pearl Harbor

My Precious Darling –

Finally arrived here yesterday afternoon late, and was mighty glad to tie up for what I hoped to be a very short while. I'm not so sure now just how long it will be as I found out a few minutes ago that somewhere between Saipan and here we lost our starboard rudder.

Darling, I'm really low in spirit. Seems as though everything and everyone is working against my coming home to you. This morning, before I knew the rudder was missing, I reported in to the Com Serv Pac operations office. We were to leave here about Thursday for S. F. – most likely with another tow. After unloading in Frisco, we are to proceed to Seattle for decommissioning. Now, that may all be changed. If we have to go into dry dock here it may be weeks before we leave. I'm fed up with the navy, the sea, and being away from you. I think I'll take my orders up Monday morning and see if there is any possible way I can have them changed and be relieved of command. Otherwise it will yet be a matter of months before I am out of service and we are together.

Sent you a telegram last night which I hope reached you this morning. I've been very lax about writing, dearest, but it wasn't because I haven't been thinking about you. I love you so very much, beautiful, and I'm sick because of the pushing around I'm getting. All the reserves who graduated last June and agreed to serve one year are being rushed home. Probably lose two of my officers when we reach Frisco if not before.

Darling, if we have to fool around much longer you'll have to come to Frisco and to hell with the money. I can't stand being away from you much longer. We're well into our tenth month apart now and I don't want any more months to pass away from the ones I love.

Also, we received practically no mail here. I got two big letters – one from Judy; one from Dad – written on March 11th. Gosh knows where all the rest has gone.

Another little bit of joy is that I can't call you because of the phone strike. All in all, darling, I'm fed up.

Sorry this is such a blue and bad news letter. Perhaps it will all work out – won't know until Monday at the earliest.

I'll write a long letter tomorrow and try and be more cheerful and newsy. I love you so darn much, darling, that I'm just about ready to say to hell with everything, sock some admiral, get a court-martial, and come home. I think it would be quicker that way.

Don't let this letter worry you, angel. I'm all right – just mad, confused, and irritated. Had to blow off steam somehow.

I adore you,

Donnie

Nearly a week later, Donald was back at sea, having left Pearl Harbor on his way to Seattle via San Francisco as originally planned. It would be just a few months before he would rejoin Mardy and their daughter. Donald had served his country well. Soon it would be time for them to begin the next chapter of their lives.

[No address information available]

Saturday Evening
April 19, 1947
at Sea

My Dearest Darling –

Last leg of the journey across this big ocean. Just about time, baby, don't you think? We got underway at six o'clock this morning, and it is really grand to not be burdened with a tow.

I received a "well done" from Commander Service Force, Pacific Fleet for the way we handled the tow. What's more important, we received the final orders that take us to Seattle for disposal. I'll be home yet, angel, though it has taken an awful long while. Don't imagine we will be in Frisco more than a few days – just long enough to unload and then on to Seattle – the end of the line thank goodness.

Keep your fingers crossed that we have no more engine trouble. I'm hoping this will be a pleasant and speedy voyage.

Also yesterday I received a letter from you which made our departure just that more joyful and complete in itself. Gosh, darling, but I'm anxious to start our new life.

Darling, I'm a little tired. The first day at sea is always a long and tedious one. I love you with all my heart. Give T'Nooker a big kiss from her daddy.

Yours Forever,
Donnie

[No address information available]

Wednesday Evening
April 23, 1947
at Sea

My Dearest Darling –

Just eleven hundred miles from the U.S.A.* – how I wish it were just that distance between you and I, darling. Nevertheless, we no longer have this big old ocean separating us. Soon nothing and no one will ever separate us again. It will be a joyous day for which I have waited a long while.

Thus far the weather has been quite favorable, though it has become cold during the past 24 hours. The first two days were gorgeous, but too much so to last. No engine trouble thus far!

Don't know just how long we will remain in Frisco, but doubt if our stay will exceed a week. I believe they will unload us speedily and send us on our way – our final voyage and I will be ever so glad to have that final voyage end. Have no concrete idea as to what decommissioning will entail nor the length of time it will take. Could be anywhere from one week to two months, but I'll settle for the former.

I have heard nothing more on this damn telephone strike, but I have my fingers crossed that it has or will have been settled before another week has passed.

Darling, can you give me some idea of how much money we have in our checking account? I should be able to bolster it quite a bit, as I understand I'll receive $300 mustering out pay just like a reserve! Of course there are small matters like three years of income taxes to be paid. They won't be particularly bad, however.

Time for the movie, lover. Will add to this tomorrow.

I love you,

Donnie

---

*Hawaii, a United States territory at the time, didn't become a state until 1959.[1]

CHAPTER TWENTY

Homecoming

According to newspaper clippings found with Donald's papers, the *LST-642* arrived at the Puget Sound naval shipyard in Seattle, Washington, on May 28, 1947. Although she had been decommissioned in late June, she was to join a group of cargo ships and an ice breaker and leave Seattle for Point Barrow, Alaska at the end of July to deliver supplies for workers on the Navy's Arctic petroleum reserve—her final journey. Donald would not be making the trip. At long last, it was time for him to come home.

In this last surviving letter from Donald to Mardy, four years of service, sacrifice, and separation were summed up in his first paragraph.

DE Storey, Lieut, USN
USS LST 642
c/o FPO, San Francisco, Calif.

Mrs. D.E. Storey
Starrs Plain Rd., RFD #2
Danbury
Connecticut
c/o Stickles

Monday Evening
June 23, 1947

My Dearest Darling –

I know this is going to be the longest week of my life. Today seemed as though it would never end. Darling, we've both waited such a long time – it's almost as though a dream were about to come true.

Lover baby, I hope you will write me a letter this week. Not talking to you is going to be hard to bear, but it's time we started saving our pennies, although I don't know of any better use than talking to you that the pennies can be put to.

Spent a very hectic day, and I'm thankful that there are but six more of the same. This past month has almost been more than I could handle. Trying to do ten things at once doesn't work – I really know that now. However, everything that was supposed to have been done is or shortly will be accomplished. We came out of dry dock tonight and now have two good propellers and rudders and a bow sheathed in wood for protection against the ice. This is the first time in my life that I've ever felt that I really need a vacation. Everyone will probably think I'm awful if I don't go to work right away, but for sixty days I'm still being paid by "Uncle", and I'm going to take my time, look around, and spend every minute with you and T'Nooker.

Received a very wonderful letter from your Dad the other day. I can't wait to sit down with my "second" mom and dad and my best girl for one of those ten o'clock specials – coffee royals and all.

Beautiful, the future is really good to look at. I have no qualms about the outside world. It may be tough, but I'll always manage to earn a living for us whether the medium be brain or brawn.

Well, darling, another ten or eleven days and we'll be together again to start what I hope and pray will always be a happy life for you.

Goodnight, sweetheart. I love you with all my heart.

Your,

Donnie

Epilogue

On June 30, 1947, Lieutenant Donald Edgar Storey reported at the U.S. Naval Receiving Station in Seattle, Washington, and completed his civil readjustment process. He was detached on July 1, and ordered to proceed to his home. His resignation was officially accepted on August 30.

He and Mardy settled in Fairfield, Connecticut, with their daughter Margery (Marcy), and welcomed two sons to their family: Christopher in 1949, and Donald Jr. in 1950.

Donald was appointed to the United States Naval Reserve in September 1948 and was honorably discharged from the service in 1956.

He found work as a sales manager for the Bassick Company in Bridgeport, Connecticut, a manufacturer of casters and automotive hardware. When he began taking the train each day to the company's headquarters in New York City, Mardy, accompanied by the children, would drive him to and from the station—just as he imagined in his letter of August 6, 1945.

As a suburban post-war American family, they enjoyed the simple things in life: playing sports, swimming, tennis, and going to football games at Yale Bowl in New Haven. In the summers, they would frequent the local beach club. And in a scene reminiscent of a Norman Rockwell painting, Sundays would find them watching football while a roast cooked in the oven. "They were loving people, fun, and great parents," said Don Jr. "We didn't have a lot of money, but we had everything we needed."

Donald kept his vow to never be apart from Mardy again. They enjoyed going to dances and dinner parties, and were active in their community. Marcy described her father as "athletic, attractive, and a gentleman always," and her mother as "very social with lots of friends." Donald's World War II service was seldom discussed with the children.

According to their son Chris, Donald was the shy one and Mardy the outgoing one in the relationship. Chris said the most important lesson his parents taught him and his siblings was to be gentle: "They personified being an example of the right person to be."

Donald, Mardy, and the children continued to enjoy summers at the family vacation retreat in upstate New York. "It was a place they both loved," said Marcy. "We've all grown up there and our kids are the fourth generation to be there. We will keep it going—it's our legacy."

As the years went on, Donald and Mardy rented a beach house every summer on Cape Cod, which evolved to a compound housing multiple generations. They became grandparents to eight, and to date, are great grandparents to twelve.

They lived in Fairfield for nearly forty years, before retiring to Cape Cod in 1986. After twenty happy years there, Donald passed away on March 4, 2007, from Alzheimer's disease.

In the final years of his life, despite his Alzheimer's, Donald's love for Mardy never waned. Marcy remembers one holiday meal when her father had just started to not be himself: "He stood up at the dining room table right in the middle of everything and toasted my mom, and said 'You are the most beautiful woman and I love you,' and he started to get teary."

When Don Jr. and his wife Vicky retired and moved to North Carolina in 2015, Mardy went with them and spent the rest of her days in their care. She died on Thanksgiving Day, November 23, 2017, at the age of 94. Donald and Mardy's ashes are buried near each other in a Cape Cod churchyard, forever together after almost 64 years of marriage.

While giving his father's eulogy in 2007, Chris Storey quoted from Tom Brokaw's book *The Greatest Generation*. Brokaw wrote that after the war ended, the celebrations were joyous, but short lived.[1] Chris took exception to that: "Mom and Dad's celebration was not short lived. It never seemed to end."

It can never be known just how many romances were kindled during World War II. Many flourished and survived after the war, but many were extinguished because of separation or the ultimate sacrifice.

Donald and Mardy's love story pays tribute to all of them.

Acknowledgments

First and foremost, I am grateful for Margery Storey, who lovingly saved these letters for so many years. Without her and Donald, there surely would be no book. To the Storey children, Chris, Don, and Marcy, thank you for entrusting me with this project and allowing me to put your parents' private thoughts and words into print. I am happy that multiple Storey generations will know them and the time they lived in through these letters.

Without my friends, family, college girls, and colleagues, some of whom are named here, I would not have made it very far. Thank you for your support and for sharing your knowledge, insight, and connections. I am grateful for all of you.

Thank you to A. J. Logan, who combed through census reports and other information to find the Storey family early on in this project. Thank you to Nanette Maxim for connecting me with A. J. and his talent for genealogy.

In 2017, law student intern Sara Bonaiuto and her supervising attorney Andy Corea at the University of Connecticut Intellectual Property and Entrepreneurship Law Clinic took on the task of preparing my copyright license agreement. I am immensely grateful to both of you for your generosity and time. Thank you to Ashleigh Backman, Esq., for recommending this wonderful resource to me.

The editorial and writing talents of Catharine Smith were indispensable. I am grateful for all the time you spent with me to rework and improve the first draft of the manuscript.

To my beta readers Mike Boissonneault, Eileen Rafferty Broderick, Melissa Reed, D. Manning Richards, Diane Smith, and Mary Lee Weber, thank you for your time, insight, and contributions.

Thank you to U.S. Navy veteran Michael Tate, for helping me find answers to my questions related to submarines and serving in the Navy, and thank you to Rosanne Torrenti for your sage advice regarding graphic design for the book. It truly does take a village.

To the great team at Elite Authors, who created the cover design and layout, and helped make the publication of this book a reality, I appreciate you.

And last, but certainly not least, to my husband, Joe Franco, thank you so much for your infinite support of me during the many years I worked on this project, and throughout our forty-one years of marriage.

Notes

Introduction

1. Kimberly Guise, "Mail Call: Letters from the Archives," The National WWII Museum New Orleans (website), March 7, 2018, https://www.nationalww2museum.org/war/articles/mail-call-letters-archives.

Chapter One

1. "U.S. Naval Academy, Bancroft Hall, Annapolis, Anne Arundel County, MD," Library of Congress, accessed January 18, 2021, http://www.loc.gov/pictures/item/md0916/.
2. Wolfgang Wild, "Sock-hops of the '40's and '50's," considerable.com, accessed January 18, 2021, https://www.considerable.com/entertainment/retronaut/sock-hops-vintage-photos/.
3. "*Honky Tonk* (1941)," DearMrGable.com, accessed January 19, 2021, http://dearmrgable.com/?page_id=4038.
4. "*A Yank in the R.A.F.* (1941)," imdb.com, accessed January 19, 2021, https://www.imdb.com/title/tt0034405/.
5. "Betty Grable – Frank Powolny 1943," TIME 100 Photos (website), accessed January 19, 2021, http://100photos.time.com/photos/betty-grable-frank-powolny.
6. Larry Spencer, "A Short History of the Rio Grande Southern Railroad & The Galloping Goose," The Galloping Goose Historical Society of Dolores, Inc. (website), accessed January 19, 2021, http://www.galloping-goose5.org/history.

7   Randy Wayne, "As Time Goes By and Albert Einstein – Do the Fundamental Things Still Apply?," *The Lansing Star*, November 20, 2015, https://www.lansingstar.com/around-town/12214-as-time-goes-by-and-albert-einstein.

8   "Armed Forces Radio Service 1942–1977" (Bing on Radio), *Bing Magazine* (website), accessed January 20, 2021, https://www.bingmagazine.co.uk.

9   John Cohassey, "Gene Krupa," Gene Krupa Reference Page, *Contemporary Musicians*, December 1994, Vol. 13, https://gkrp.net/biographies/gene-krupa/.

10   "Carvel Hall – A Showcase of Colonial Charm," Historic Annapolis (website), accessed January 20, 2021, https://annapolis.org/media-content/carvel-hall—a-showcase-colonial-charm.

11   *Merriam-Webster.com Dictionary*, s.v. "June Week," accessed January 20, 2021, https://www.merriam-webster.com/dictionary/June%20Week.

12   The Editors of Encyclopaedia Britannica, "Walter Winchell," *Encyclopaedia Britannica*, April 3, 2020, https://www.britannica.com/biography/Walter-Winchell.

Chapter Two

1   "Consolidated PBY-Catalina," Smithsonian Institution National Air and Space Museum, transferred from the United States Navy, accessed January 20, 2021, https://airandspace.si.edu/collection-objects/consolidated-pby-5-catalina/nasm_A19730277000.

2   "USS Gatling DD-671 – 1943 Condensed Ship's Log," USS Gatling Reunion Association, February 14, 2013, http://www.destroyers.org/uss-gatling/DD671_1943%20ships%20log.htm.

3   *Dictionary.com*, s.v. "Sou," https://www.dictionary.com/browse/sou.

Chapter Three

1   "USS Gatling DD-671 – 1943 Condensed Ship's Log," USS Gatling Reunion Association, February 14, 2013, http://www.destroyers.org/uss-gatling/DD671_1943%20ships%20log.htm.

2   David Hinckley, "Future of Radio Martin Block Makes Believe," *New York Daily News*, March 17, 2004, https://www.nydailynews.com/archives/news/future-radio-martin-block-article-1.630237.

3   The Vintage Record, "The History of Vinyl," American History Now, January 27, 2014, http://americanhistorynow.org/2014/01/27/the-history-of-vinyl/; Steve Mellon, "Breaking Records for the War Effort," *Pittsburgh Post-Gazette*, November 18, 2013, https://newsinteractive.post-gazette.com/thedigs/2013/11/18/breaking-records-for-the-war-effort/.

4   "USS Gatling DD-671 – 1943 Condensed Ship's Log," USS Gatling Reunion Association.

5   "USS Gatling DD-671 – 1943 Condensed Ship's Log," USS Gatling Reunion Association.

6   "USS Gatling DD-671 – 1943 Condensed Ship's Log," USS Gatling Reunion Association.

Chapter Four

1   "USS Gatling DD-671 – 1943 Condensed Ship's Log," USS Gatling Reunion Association, February 14, 2013, http://www.destroyers.org/uss-gatling/DD671_1943%20ships%20log.htm.

2   "*Blood and Sand* (1941)." imdb.com, accessed January 21, 2021, https://www.imdb.com/title/tt0033405/.

3   "USS Gatling DD-671 – 1943 Condensed Ship's Log," USS Gatling Reunion Association.

4   Harold L. Erickson, "American Broadcasting Company," *Encyclopaedia Britannica*, February 21, 2019, https://www.britannica.com/topic/American-Broadcasting-Company; "History Timeline of NBC," No Cable, accessed January 20, 2021, https://nocable.org/timeline/nbc-history.

5   "Fred Waring, a Biography," (Fred Waring's America), Pennsylvania State University Libraries, January 9, 2006, https://web.archive.org/web/20080720001210/http://www.libraries.psu.edu/waring/fwbio.html.

6   "Ship's History," USS Gatling Reunion Association, accessed January 21, 2021, http://www.destroyers.org/uss-gatling/DD671_shipshistory.htm.

Chapter Five

1   "USS Gatling DD-671 – 1944 Condensed Ship's Log," USS Gatling Reunion Association, February 14, 2013, http://www.destroyers.org/uss-gatling/DD671_1944%20ships%20log.htm.

2   Sarah Pruitt, "After Pearl Harbor: The Race to Save the U.S. Fleet," History, A & E Television Networks, LLC, December 1, 2016, https://www.history.com/news/after-pearl-harbor-the-race-to-save-the-u-s-fleet.

3   Erin Blakemore, "After Pearl Harbor, Hawaii Spent Three Years Under Martial Law," History, A & E Television Networks, LLC, August 23, 2019, www.history.com/news/hawaii-wwii-martial-law.

4   "USS Gatling DD-671 – 1944 Condensed Ship's Log," USS Gatling Reunion Association.

5   James Travers, "Watch on the Rhine (1943) Film Review", French Films.org, accessed January 27, 2021, http://www.frenchfilms.org/review/watch-on-the-rhine-1943.html.

6   "*City for Conquest* (1940)", imdb.com, accessed January 27, 2021, https://www.imdb.com/title/tt0032342/.

7   "The Daily Argus (Mount Vernon, N.Y.) 1892–1994," Library of Congress, accessed January 27, 2021, https://www.loc.gov/item/sn83031711/.

8   "USS Gatling DD-671 – 1944 Condensed Ship's Log," USS Gatling Reunion Association;
"Gatling (DD-671)," Naval History and Heritage Command, March 31, 2016, https://www.history.navy.mil/content/history/nhhc/research/histories/ship-histories/danfs/g/gatling.html.

Chapter Six

1   "USS Gatling DD-671 – 1944 Condensed Ship's Log," USS Gatling Reunion Association, February 14, 2013, http://www.destroyers.org/uss-gatling/DD671_1944%20ships%20log.htm.

2   Cale Weissman, "Behind the Strange and Controversial Ritual When

You Cross the Equator at Sea," Atlas Obscura, October 23, 2015, https://www.atlasobscura.com/articles/behind-the-strange-and-controversial-ritual-when-you-cross-the-equator-at-sea.

[3] *Merriam-Webster.com Dictionary*, s.v. "Fo'c'sle," accessed January 27, 2021, https://www.merriam-webster.com/dictionary/fo%27c%27sle.

[4] "USS Gatling DD-671 – 1944 Condensed Ship's Log," USS Gatling Reunion Association.

[5] "USS Gatling DD-671 – 1944 Condensed Ship's Log," USS Gatling Reunion Association.

[6] J. Rickard, "Operation Flintlock (31 January – 4 February 1944)," HistoryofWar.org., November 6, 2017, http://www.historyofwar.org/articles/operation_fllintlock.html.

[7] "USS Gatling DD-671 – 1944 Condensed Ship's Log," USS Gatling Reunion Association.

[8] "Letter Writing in WWII," Smithsonian National Postal Museum (website), accessed February 1, 2121, https://postalmuseum.si.edu/exhibition/victory-mail/letter-writing-in-wwii; "Victory Mail," Smithsonian National Postal Museum, accessed February 1, 2121, https://postalmuseum.si.edu/exhibition/victory-mail.

[9] Rickard, "Operation Flintlock," HistoryofWar.org.

[10] "USS Gatling DD-671 – 1944 Condensed Ship's Log," USS Gatling Reunion Association.

[11] *Merriam-Webster.com Dictionary*, s.v. "Dolt," accessed February 1, 2021, https://www.merriam-webster.com/dictionary/dolt.

Chapter Seven

[1] Tom Farrier, "What was the Most Dangerous Military Service in WW2: The Army, The Navy or the Air Force?," Quora.com, accessed February 1, 2021, https://www.quora.com/What-was-the-most-dangerous-military-service-in-WW2-the-Army-the-Navy-or-the-Air-Force.

Chapter Eight

1   Samuel J. Cox, "H-026-3: Operation Hailstone-Carrier Raid on Truk Island, 17-18 February 1944," Naval History and Heritage Command (website), May 3, 2019, https://www.history.navy.mil/about-us/leadership/director/directors-corner/h-grams/h-gram-026/H-026-3.html.

2   "USS Gatling DD-671 – 1944 Condensed Ship's Log," USS Gatling Reunion Association, February 14, 2013, http://www.destroyers.org/uss-gatling/DD671_1944%20ships%20log.htm.

3   "USS Gatling DD-671 – 1944 Condensed Ship's Log," USS Gatling Reunion Association.

4   "*The Fighting Seebees* (1944)," imdb.com, accessed February 2, 2021, https://www.imdb.com/title/tt0036824/.

5   "*Good Morning, Judge* (1943)," imdb.com, accessed February 2, 2021, https://www.imdb.com/title/tt0035950/.

6   The Editors of Encyclopaedia Britannica, "United States Presidential Election of 1944," *Encyclopaedia Britannica,* October 31, 2020, https://www.britannica.com/event/United-States-presidential-election-of-1944.

Chapter Nine

1   "Carbonero (SS-337)," (from the Dictionary of American Naval Fighting Ships), Naval History and Heritage Command, U.S. Navy, April 21, 2016, https://www.history.navy.mil/research/histories/ship-histories/danfs/c/carbonero.html.

2   Frank Freidel, "Franklin D. Roosevelt," *Encyclopaedia Britannica*, January 26, 2021, https://www.britannica.com/biography/Franklin-D-Roosevelt.

3   Joseph P. Mastrangelo, "World War II Submarine Life," *The Washington Post*, February 5, 1977, https://www.washingtonpost.com/archive/lifestyle/1977/02/05/world-war-ii-submarine-life/59c0886d-c834-42ce-a3e4-90467df8cf94/.

4   "Submarine Information and Instruction Manual, 1942," (Qualification for Submarines, 64), Submarine Division Forty-One Submarine Training Unit, San Francisco Maritime National Park Association (website),

accessed February 3, 2021, https://maritime.org/doc/s-boat/index.htm; USNUM Curator, "Submarine Dolphins," United States Naval Undersea Museum (website), January 19, 2017, https://navalunderseamuseum.org/submarine-dolphins/.

5   "Submarine Qualifications Designation for Enlisted Members," U.S. Navy, June 14, 2018, https://www.public.navy.mil/bupers-npc/reference/milpersman/1000/1200Classification/Documents/1220-040.pdf.

6   "Carbonero (SS-337)," Naval History and Heritage Command.

7   "Carbonero (SS-337)," Naval History and Heritage Command.

8   Dan Olmsted, "WWII Polls - Should We Continue Rationing Gasoline After the War?," The National World War II Museum, New Orleans (website), October 8, 2018, https://www.nationalww2museum.org/war/articles/should-we-continue-rationing-gasoline-after-war.

9   Peter Guttridge, "Obituary: Kathleen Winsor: Author of the Racy Bestseller 'Forever Amber'," May 29, 2003, *The Independent*, https://www.independent.co.uk/news/obituaries/kathleen-winsor-36575.html.

10   "Carbonero (SS-337)," Naval History and Heritage Command.

11   Biography.com Editors, "Benito Mussolini Biography," The Biography.com website, A & E Television Networks, April 29, 2014, https://www.biography.com/dictator/benito-mussolini;Christopher Klein, "Mussolini's Final Hours," History.com, April 28, 2015, https://www.history.com/news/mussolinis-final-hours.

Chapter Ten

1   Wilfrid F. Knapp et al., "Adolf Hitler," *Encyclopaedia Britannica*, April 26, 2020, https://www.britannica.com/biography/Adolf-Hitler.

2   American Merchant Marine at War, "Rights and Privileges of American Servicemen (System of Allotments and Allowances)," Office of War Information Press Release, May 23, 1943, www.usmm.org, http://www.usmm.org/wsa/rights.html.

3   "La Concha Hotel & Spa, Key West," accessed February 4, 2021, https://www.laconchakeywest.com/.

4   Margalit Fox, "Fabian Bachrach, 92, Portraitist Who Photographed

Kennedy, Dies," *The New York Times*, March 1, 2010, https://www.ny-times.com/2010/03/02/arts/design/02bachrach.html.

5   "What You Need to Know About VE Day," Imperial War Museums (website), accessed February 2, 2021, https://www.iwm.org.uk/history/what-you-need-to-know-about-ve-day.

6   John Keegan, "Normandy Invasion," *Encyclopaedia Britannica*, October 5, 2020, https://www.britannica.com/event/Normandy-Invasion.

Chapter Eleven

1   C. Peter Chen, "Carbonero Operational Timeline," World War II Database, accessed February 11, 2021, https://ww2db.com/ship_spec.php?ship_id=694.

2   "Carbonero (SS-337)," (from the Dictionary of American Naval Fighting Ships), Naval History and Heritage Command, U.S. Navy, April 21, 2016, https://www.history.navy.mil/research/histories/ship-histories/danfs/c/carbonero.html.

3   "Carbonero (SS-337)," Naval History and Heritage Command.

4   John Glover, "Warsaw Concerto," Los Angeles Philharmonic Association (website), July, 2007, https://www.laphil.com/musicdb/pieces/4639/warsaw-concerto.

Chapter Twelve

1   "Carbonero (SS-337)," (from the Dictionary of American Naval Fighting Ships), Naval History and Heritage Command, U.S. Navy, April 21, 2016, https://www.history.navy.mil/research/histories/ship-histories/danfs/c/carbonero.html.

2   "Carbonero (SS-337)," Naval History and Heritage Command.

3   Manning Garrett, "The Japanese Government Pesos," Antiquemoney.com, accessed February 11, 2021, http://www.antiquemoney.com/the-japanese-government-pesos/; "WWII Japanese Invasion Money," Educationalcoin.com, accessed February 11, 2021, https://www.educationalcoin.com/media/amfile/files/(1)imagesalbumsoptjimalb.pdf.

4   The Editors of Encyclopaedia Britannica, "Olongapo," June 26, 2020, *Encyclopaedia Britannica*, https://www.britannica.com/place/Olongapo.

5   *Whistling in Dixie* (1942), imdb.com, https://www.imdb.com/title/tt0035552/.

Chapter Thirteen

1   "Carbonero (SS-337)," (from the Dictionary of American Naval Fighting Ships), Naval History and Heritage Command, U.S. Navy, April 21, 2016, https://www.history.navy.mil/research/histories/ship-histories/danfs/c/carbonero.html.

2   The Editors of Encyclopaedia Britannica, "Atomic Bomb," *Encyclopaedia Britannica*, August 27, 2020, https://www.britannica.com/technology/atomic-bomb.

3   MC1 Ryan Litzenberger, "First Filipina Female Submarine Officer Earns Dolphins Aboard USS Ohio," *The Flagship*, Military Newspapers of Virginia, June 11, 2020, https://www.militarynews.com/norfolk-navy-flagship/first-filipina-female-submarine-officer-earns-dolphins-aboard-uss-ohio/article_42b95cbc-a9af-11ea-ac03-67aa7045c6ca.html.

4   Takeshi Toyoda et al., "Japan (World War II and Defeat)," *Encyclopaedia Britannica*, February 9, 2021, https://www.britannica.com/place/Japan/World-War-II-and-defeat.

5   The Editors of Encyclopaedia Britannica, "Atomic Bomb."

6   "Carbonero (SS-337)," Naval History and Heritage Command.

7   Takeshi Toyoda et al., "Japan (World War II and Defeat)," *Encyclopaedia Britannica*.

8   History.com Editors, "V-J Day," History, A & E Television Networks, LLC, October 14, 2009, https://www.history.com/topics/world-war-ii/v-j-day.

Chapter Fourteen

1   "Carbonero (SS-337)," (from the Dictionary of American Naval Fighting Ships), Naval History and Heritage Command, U.S. Navy, April 21, 2016, https://www.history.navy.mil/research/histories/ship-histories/danfs/c/carbonero.html.

2　"What Does ALNAV Mean?" Acronyms And Slang, accessed February 16, 2021, http://acronymsandslang.com/definition/11394/ALNAV-meaning.html.

3　Chris Chiel and Julie Decker, *Quonset Hut: Metal Living for the Modern Age* (New York: Princeton Architectural Press, 2005), Amazon.com book summary, https://www.amazon.com/Quonset-Hut-Metal-Living-Modern/dp/1568985193.

Chapter Fifteen

1　Adrian R. Lewis, "Landing ship, tank (LST)," *Encyclopaedia Britannica*, October 12, 2016, https://www.britannica.com/technology/landing-ship-tank.

2　"LST-642," (from the Dictionary of American Naval Fighting Ships), Naval History and Heritage Command, Department of the Navy – Naval Historical Center, accessed February 16, 2021, http://web.archive.org/web/20140728034630/http://www.history.navy.mil/danfs/l21/lst-642.htm.

3　"GHQ," *COBUILD Advanced English Dictionary*, HarperCollins Publishers, accessed February 18, 2021, https://www.collinsdictionary.com/us/dictionary/english/ghq#:~:text=GHQ%20is%20used%20to%20refer,'.

4　Mark Schlabach, "Blanchard More Than Football Hero," ESPN, April 20, 2009, https://www.espn.com/college-football/columns/story?columnist=schlabach_mark&id=4083530.

5　"The Road Films: Bob Hope and Bing Crosby," American Masters: Bing Crosby Rediscovered, PBS-WNET, accessed February 18, 2021, https://www.pbs.org/wnet/americanmasters/bing-crosby-the-road-films-bob-hope-and-bing-crosby/3544/.

6　"Landing Craft, Mechanized and Utility – LCM/LCU," U.S. Navy (website), January 17, 2019, https://www.navy.mil/Resources/Fact-Files/Display-FactFiles/Article/2171588/landing-craft-mechanized-and-utility-lcmlcu/.

7   The Editors of Encyclopaedia Britannica, "Alan Ladd," *Encyclopaedia Britannica*, January 25, 2021, https://www.britannica.com/biography/Alan-Ladd.

Chapter Sixteen

1   E. Tillotson, "Japanese Earthquake of December 21, 1946," *Nature*, January 11, 1947, 72, https://www.nature.com/articles/159072a0.pdf?origin=ppub.

Chapter Seventeen

1   Myrna Oliver, "Ginny Simms; Singer, Radio Personality," *Los Angeles Times,* April 6, 1994, https://www.latimes.com/archives/la-xpm-1994-04-06-mn-42689-story.html.

2   *Destry Rides Again* (1939), imdb.com, accessed February 20, 2021, https://www.imdb.com/title/tt0031225/.

3   The Editors of Encyclopaedia Britannica, "Saipan," *Encyclopaedia Britannica*, August 27, 2012, https://www.britannica.com/place/Saipan.

4   "LSM Landing Ship, Medium," GlobalSecurity.org (website), accessed February 20, 2021, https://www.globalsecurity.org/military/systems/ship/lsm.htm.

5   *Notorious* (1946), imdb.com, accessed February 20, 2021, https://www.imdb.com/title/tt0038787/.

Chapter Eighteen

1   Kenneth C. Davis, *Don't Know Much About History* (New York: Crown Publishers, 1990), 321.

2   "Truman Doctrine," Lexico.com, accessed February 22, 2021, https://www.lexico.com/en/definition/truman_doctrine.

Chapter Nineteen

1   "Hawaii Becomes a State," America's Story from America's Library, Library of Congress, accessed February 22, 2021, http://www.americaslibrary.gov/jb/modern/jb_modern_hawaii_1.html.

Epilogue

1   Tom Brokaw, *The Greatest Generation* (New York: Random House, 1998), XXVII-XXVIII.

About the Author

Author photograph by Io Escu Smith – AG Productions.

Lisa Franco has been telling people's stories for more than four decades. As a writer/producer for the ABC television affiliate WTNH 8 in New Haven, Connecticut, she earned multiple Emmy nominations and journalism awards for her documentaries. She also served as public affairs director for the station before she became the state communications director for one of the largest nonprofit organizations in the country.

While Lisa's background includes marketing, media relations, and public relations, these days she is a freelance writer and owner of Over the Moon Vintage, an online collectibles shop.

Lisa's parents were members of the Greatest Generation, and her father, Nino Maurizi, was a World War II Army Air Corps veteran. She attributes this to her interest in the war and the loving relationships that developed during that period in our history.

Lisa and her husband, Joe, live in Connecticut and are the proud parents of their sixth rescue dog, Maggie.

www.linkedin.com/in/lisafranco

Made in the USA
Middletown, DE
06 January 2023

21513882R00187